PROPHECY

IN LIGHT OF

TODAY

PROPHECY

IN LIGHT OF

TODAY

CHARLES H. DYER
MARK BAILEY
ERWIN W. LUTZER
LARRY MERCER
SAMUEL NAAMAN
MICHAEL RYDELNIK

ISBN: 0-8024-1357-9

1 3 5 7 9 10 8 6 4 2
Printed in the United States of America

To Dr & Mrs Mitchell

with honor

This book is dedicated to the Board of Trustees at Moody Bible Institute,
the Board of Elders at Moody Church,
and the Board of Incorporate Members at Dallas Theological Seminary.
These are choice servants of Christ
who provide wise counsel and leadership
at the ministries where the different contributors to this volume serve.
These board members unselfishly sacrifice their time,
their talents, and their treasure
to advance God's work here on earth.
They are colleagues and friends . . .
but even more, they are wise and godly advisers
who richly deserve our praise and gratitude.

By wisdom a house is built, and through understanding it is established;
Through knowledge its rooms are filled with rare and beautiful treasures.
A wise man has great power, and a man of knowledge increases strength;
For waging war you need guidance, and for victory many advisers.
—Proverbs 24:3–6

Thanks for your years of
support + contribution to
the DTS family + Board.

Mark L. Bailey
Phil 1:21

CONTENTS

FOREWORD: THE NEW 911

Dr. Joseph M. Stowell

On Friday, January 12, 1968, AT&T held a press conference in Washington, D.C., to announce their designation of 911 as a universal emergency number. Though it took years for the emergency number to be implemented nationally, 911 became synonymous with disasters, emergencies, and urgent cries for help.

After the fall 2001 airplane hijackings and terrorist attacks against the World Trade Center and Pentagon, 911 took on still another meaning because that is the date (9/11) when those horrific events happened. The date will forever be lodged in the collective consciousness of those Americans who survived the vicious attacks . . . and those who watched it unfold on television.

The new 911 reminded Americans that we are vulnerable to attack . . . that the world remains a dangerous place . . . that our lives can suddenly and irreversibly be altered by events beyond our control. But the events also reminded us that we must depend on God and His Word for guidance and direction in uncertain times. The president of the United States offered comfort and hope to a grieving nation by quoting Scripture. Billy Graham used God's Word to remind us that God is still on His throne. Even when we can't understand what is happening—or why—He remains in control. Those who have a personal faith in Jesus Christ also came to understand in a new way how "in all things God works for the good" (Romans 8:28), even when the "all things" include events caused by evil men who desire to inflict hurt and harm.

But most of all, the events of 911 reminded Christians that this life is temporary and fleeting . . . and that our hope reaches beyond this life to eternity. We also caught glimpses of how God might bring about His promised program for the future . . . using Islam's hatred for Israel and the West, and our desire for a strong military leader who will arise to offer peace and safety.

At Moody Bible Institute, we believe that God does control the future and that He has given us a broad outline of what tomorrow holds. He did this to give us hope . . . and to keep us stable in times of stress and uncertainty. This book is written to help you understand what the Bible does say about the future. Using the events of the new 911 as a springboard, the different authors will guide you through various aspects of God's plan for this world.

Each of the six writers is a trusted friend and faithful colleague in ministry. Four serve on the faculty of Moody Bible Institute, one is senior pastor of Moody Church, and one is president of Dallas Theological Seminary. They all write with unity, clarity, and passion as they share the significance of prophecy for today.

Read through the following pages with an active mind, a prayerful heart . . . and an open Bible. Gain insight into God's plans for the future. And discover that events today could be setting the stage for Christ's soon return.

1 A PEACE TO END ALL PEACE

Dr. Charles H. Dyer

THE ELUSIVE SEARCH FOR PEACE

The twentieth century was not kind to those who hoped it would usher in an era of world peace. As the century began, the false belief that the world was evolving into a better place united with the biblical teaching of a kingdom of righteousness . . . and many proclaimed that humanity was already creating its own kingdom of God on earth.

This idea that the message of God's love and peace was about to sweep the world was captured in the words of the song written by H. Ernest Nichol in 1896.

> We've a story to tell to the nations that shall turn their hearts to the right,
> A story of truth and mercy, a story of peace and light, a story of peace and light.

For the darkness shall turn to dawning, and the
dawning to noonday bright,
And Christ's great kingdom shall come to earth, the
kingdom of love and light.

Less than two decades into the new century the hoped-for peace was shattered by World War I. Yet since it was called "the war to end all wars," one senses people still believed that once it was fought, peace would finally come to the world. Unfortunately, "the war to end all wars" didn't live up to its name.

The final eight decades of the twentieth century were a string of wars—from the worldwide conflagration of World War II to the brutal regional conflicts that continue to erupt in Africa, Central America, and the Middle East. The periods between were punctuated with atrocities and horrors . . . from the Holocaust against the Jewish people to the genocide in Russia, China, and parts of Africa, to the legalized murder of millions of unborn children around the world.

The threat of nuclear annihilation began at the end of World War II. The danger of the world's superpowers launching thousands of nuclear warheads against each other has diminished. But it has been replaced with the equally unsettling threat of rogue states or extremist groups building or acquiring nuclear weapons . . . and setting them off in major cities around the world. Add to this the old—but suddenly new—danger posed by chemical and biological weapons, and we have a world that has entered a new century and a new millennium, with a collective anxiety disorder.

The world is still searching for global peace. When the United Nations was established, it inscribed a quotation from Isaiah on its new building in New York City: "They shall beat their swords into plowshares, and their spears into pruninghooks" (Isaiah 2:4 KJV). But the world still has too many swords and spears, and too few plowshares and pruning hooks. Will the world ever achieve a peace to end all peace? The search is still on as today's headlines make abundantly clear. And yet, one truth has emerged—punctuated so forcefully when four airplanes smashed into the World Trade Centers, the Pentagon, and a field in Pennsylvania—peace will only come when evil is vanquished.

The world should expect to encounter more potholes on the road to peace. Vice President Dick Cheney expressed it well when he warned, "We have to assume there will be more attacks. These changes we have made are permanent, at least in the lifetimes of most of us." President Bush sounded a sober note to the world when he said, "These terrorist groups seek to destabilize entire nations and regions. They're seeking chemical, biological, and nuclear weapons. Given the means, our enemies would be a threat to every nation and eventually to civilization itself."

These statements, though true, were also unsettling. America had been isolated from much of the world's turmoil, but evil had now struck in a dramatic way on our own shores. *Time* magazine said, "The federal agencies that people are counting on to ensure their safety are struggling to meet a challenge unlike any other in living memory. What more needs to be done and does America have the political will to make it happen?" We want peace, but are we willing to pay the price required to obtain it?

LESSONS FROM SEPTEMBER 11

I see four lessons that have pushed their way to the forefront since September 11. Each is unique, yet they are all interwoven. Each is not terribly significant when seen in isolation, but viewed together they paint a picture that is remarkably similar to a portrait painted in God's Word of the time that precedes Christ's return to earth.

Lesson 1: People Adapt to Changing Realities

The first lesson is that people quickly adapt to new realities when their present reality is shattered. A dramatic example of this occurred in Amherst, Massachusetts. On Monday evening, September 10, the Select Board of Amherst voted four to one to prevent twenty-nine American flags from flying downtown for an extended period of time. They limited the time when the flags could be flown to six holiday periods. Why? Because many in this politically correct, liberal college town felt that flying the flag made the town look "too American." A professor from the University of Massachusetts addressed the Select Board and declared that, "The flag is a symbol of tyranny and fear and destruction and terrorism."

The next day the terrorist attacks on New York City and Washington, D.C., took place. As the horror of those attacks unfolded, a group of individuals, including some from the Amherst Department of Public Works, located the flags, took them downtown, and reattached them to the light poles. The *Daily Hampshire Gazette* quoted one of the men who had been involved in the meeting the evening of September 10 . . . and who then helped put the flags back up. He said, "It's strange how one day can make a difference." What was politically correct in Amherst on September 10 was politically incorrect the next day. Amazing, isn't it? Events can dramatically change over the course of a single day . . . and people will adapt to these new realities.

Lesson 2: People Will Unite to Face a Common Threat

The second lesson that has surfaced since September 11 is that people will unite to face a common fear or a common foe. Before September 11, flags were out of fashion; after September 11, they were out of stock because so many people wanted to purchase them to show their pride in the United States. Red, white, and blue became the colors of choice . . . even for M&M candy! "God Bless America" and "The Star Spangled Banner" took on new meaning as they rang out across the steps of the Capitol . . . and at sporting events and patriotic gatherings across the country. A nation that was fractured and divided following the presidential election became, at least on the surface, very united once again. Things can change very rapidly.

Lesson 3: People Will Give Up Freedom to Gain Security

A third lesson that has surfaced since September 11 is that people will give up freedom to gain security. Congress enacted legislation following the terrorist attacks to enhance security and expand the government's ability to root out terrorists. But those same laws could be used against citizens who are not terrorists. Anyone who has flown in an airplane since September 11 has experienced longer lines, the presence of armed military personnel, and the inconvenience of random searches. Yet few complain, because these restrictions are seen as the only way to guarantee passenger safety. Americans demand their freedom until their personal safety is threatened. And then, for the sake of security, most will willingly give up some of their freedom.

Lesson 4: People Want Strong Leaders in Times of Crisis

The fourth lesson to surface since September 11 is that people want—and will follow—a strong leader in times of crisis. On November 12, 2001, an article appeared in the *Chicago Tribune* with detailed information on who really won the election for president in Florida . . . the previous November! Amazingly, few even cared. The issue that had gripped America for months—and that had cast a shadow over the first eight months of George Bush's presidency—no longer mattered. After September 11 America united solidly behind its president. In times of crisis people want, and will follow, a leader who stands up and takes responsibility; and President Bush rose to that challenge.

LET'S PLAY CLUE

The world desperately wants "a peace to end all peace." And that desire will someday prompt people to give up personal freedom and follow a strong leader who will rise up and promise to lead the world toward peace. The Bible predicts the rise of a man who is going to promise peace and yet plunge the world into a time of evil and war unparalleled in history. Events since September 11 can provide psychological insight into how this future Antichrist will arise . . . and how an unsuspecting world will follow him.

In 1949 Parker Brothers introduced the British board game Cleudo to America and called it Clue. The board has pictures on it that represent the different rooms in a fictitious mansion. The object of the game is to solve the mystery of the untimely death of Mr. Body. Players roll dice to move between the rooms on the game board. Once a player enters a room, he or she can make "suggestions" about the who, the what, and the where of the crime. "I suggest the crime was committed by [you suggest the individual], and was committed with [you suggest the weapon], and was committed in [you suggest the room you have entered]." Through the process of elimination, each player tries to deduce the who, what, and where for the crime. Finally, one player feels confident enough to make an "accusation." That player then opens the case file, a small packet that contains the three cards, to see if he or she is correct. The first to guess all three correctly wins the game. Indeed, it *was* Professor Plum; he *did* use the revolver; and it *did* happen in the dining room!

In some ways, studying what the Bible says about the

identity and activity of the future Antichrist is very similar to playing Clue. The Bible clearly teaches that God is in control of world events. He was in control on September 11, He is in control now, and He will be in control tomorrow. The events of the world are moving toward the ultimate return of Jesus Christ to this earth to set up His kingdom.

Jesus told His disciples that no one would know the day or the hour of His return (Matthew 24:36). His words should cause us to be cautious about reading too much into current events. People have erred in the past when they stood up to say, "We are now in the end times." To set dates is unwise. But, Jesus also said in Matthew 24 that His followers should learn the lesson of the fig tree: "As soon as its twigs get tender and its leaves come out, you know that summer is near. Even so, when you see all these things, you know that it is near, right at the door" (vv. 32–33). Though cautioning His disciples against setting dates, Jesus did encourage them to pay close attention to what is happening in the world and to evaluate current events by the steady light of God's Word. When events in the world begin to parallel the predicted events in God's Word, it could signal that the end times are indeed drawing closer.

So, what are the clues that can help us identify the Antichrist? Does the Bible present enough information on the *who,* the *what,* and the *where* to help us paint an identifiable portrait of this coming evil world leader? Using the Bible as our playing board, let's enter several of its rooms to see if we can discover the necessary clues.

Who?

The room in God's Word where we begin is the book of 2 Thessalonians. Here we turn over the first Clue card to discover the *who.* This is Paul's second letter to a church that he had only visited for a few weeks. Very early in his second missionary journey, Paul planted a church at Thessalonica in what is today northern Greece (cf. Acts 17:1–10). Paul was forced to flee from Thessalonica because of persecution. Shortly after leaving, he wrote his first letter to this group of faithful saints. Then, after receiving a distressing report from the church, he wrote back the letter we now call 2 Thessalonians. Though the church was young, Paul felt it was very important for its people to understand what the future held.

In 2 Thessalonians 2, Paul reminded the people about "the coming of our Lord Jesus Christ and our being gathered to him" (v. 1). This was familiar ground because Paul had addressed the topic in his first letter (1 Thessalonians 4:14–18). Paul returned to the subject by encouraging the Thessalonian believers "not to become easily unsettled or alarmed by some prophecy, report or letter supposed to have come from us, saying that the day of the Lord has already come" (2 Thessalonians 2:2). Evidently, someone had visited or written to the Thessalonians and told them that Paul had announced the beginning of the Day of the Lord. The implication was that the Antichrist had appeared and that the church was now going through the Tribulation period. Paul didn't know if someone had forged a letter that was supposedly from him or if an individual had delivered a false report saying that a prophecy had been given to Paul. The apostle sought to encourage the Thessalonians, so they would not be upset, by explaining to them what the future held. Paul focused in a special way on the person often called the Antichrist, and he made six key points about this future world leader.

He will be a man of lawlessness. Paul referred to the Antichrist as "the man of lawlessness," and he reminded his audience that the Day of the Lord could not come until this evil leader is revealed (v. 3). By identifying the Antichrist as a man of lawlessness, Paul emphasized that he will set himself in opposition to all that God says is good and right. When we hear the word "Antichrist," we usually assume that the prefix "anti" indicates that this individual will actively oppose Jesus Christ. But the Greek word *anti* can also mean "instead of" or "in place of." Likely, both ideas apply to this person. That is, he is someone who will set himself in place of Jesus Christ and who will also actively oppose all that God has decreed to be right. He will embody the spirit of lawlessness and rebellion that will characterize the end times.

He will exalt himself. Paul then adds a second characteristic of this future leader. "He will oppose and will exalt himself over everything that is called God or is worshiped, so that he sets himself up in God's temple, proclaiming himself to be God" (v. 4). The Antichrist will exalt himself as God . . . and he will do so in God's own temple in Jerusalem. Though this is a dramatic announcement, it was not entirely new or unique to Paul. Daniel 9:27 predicted the rise of an evil "prince" who first confirms a covenant with Israel only to break the agreement midway through the seven-year period and set up "an abomination that causes desolation." In Matthew 24 Jesus gave His disciples a glimpse into future events that would climax with His return to earth. "So when you see standing in the holy place 'the abomination that causes desolation,' spoken of through the prophet Daniel—let the reader understand—then let those who are in Judea flee to the mountains" (vv. 15–16). Daniel, Jesus, and Paul all focused on the same event . . . and that event is still future. The Antichrist will be clearly identified when he walks into the temple in Jerusalem and declares himself to be God.

God is currently restraining his appearance. Paul reveals his third characteristic in verses 6–8 of 2 Thessalonians 2: "And now you know what is holding him back, so that he may be revealed at the proper time. For the secret power of lawlessness is already at work; but the one who now holds it back will continue to do so till he is taken out of the way. And then the lawless one will be revealed." The appearance of the Antichrist is now being held back by God's power, but God will allow this individual to be revealed at the proper time. Many Americans have been living their lives in fear since the events of September 11. We don't know what tomorrow holds. We don't know what could happen. Some are afraid to open their mail or fly on an airplane, or even to enter a tall building. But this verse reminds us that God is in control. Evil cannot reach beyond any barriers God chooses to erect.

As bad as the world is today, it could be worse. But God is holding evil in check. The "one who now holds [him] back" has been understood to refer to the Holy Spirit or to the church as empowered by the Holy Spirit. When Paul says that the one holding evil back is going to be taken out of the way, he could be referring to the time when God will remove the church from the earth, or to the time when God's Spirit will cease to restrain evil. In either case, a day will come when God will allow evil to run unchecked in this world, but that day has not yet begun.

His time will be limited. Having just assured his readers that the Antichrist will not appear until God withdraws His hand from restraining evil, Paul very quickly adds that the Antichrist's time for exercising his evil rule will be limited. This lawless leader is the one "whom the Lord Jesus will overthrow with the breath of his mouth and destroy by the splendor of his coming" (2 Thessalonians 2:8). The Antichrist cannot appear until God grants permission, and he cannot continue beyond the time of Christ's second coming. Paul's message parallels the promise of Daniel 11. After describing the activity of this final man of evil (Daniel 11:36–45a), the prophet predicts that "he will come to his end, and no one will help him" (v. 45b). He will be destroyed in God's time . . . through the power of God alone.

Nearly a half century after the apostle Paul wrote to the church of Thessalonica, the apostle John provided additional revelation about the final end of this Man of Sin. In Revelation 19, John describes the final battle where the Antichrist and his forces unite to oppose the God of heaven. But instead of some great battle, John records that a sword comes out of Jesus' mouth and destroys the Antichrist's army. The Antichrist and his lieutenant, the False Prophet, are seized and thrown immediately into the lake of fire. The forces of evil, led by the Antichrist and supported by Satan and all the powers of darkness, are no match for the power of God. Paul wanted to remind his readers—and us—that God is going to win in the end. Don't get discouraged!

His power comes from Satan. Paul's fifth characteristic that helps identify the Antichrist is the source of his power. "The coming of the lawless one will be in accordance with the work of Satan" (2 Thessalonians 2:9a). The Antichrist will rise to prominence and be successful because he will be empowered by Satan. Satan will marshal the demonic forces of hell and use them to accomplish his plan through this individual. When the Antichrist rises to power, he will seem to have wisdom and power far beyond that of mere mortals. He will be able to do great deeds because Satan will be at work through him.

He will try to deceive the world. The sixth characteristic Paul lists is that the arrival of the Antichrist will be accompanied by "all kinds of counterfeit miracles, signs and wonders, and in every sort of evil that deceives those who are perishing" (vv. 9b–10a). Satan will use counterfeit miracles, convincing signs, and supernatural wonders in an attempt to deceive everyone in the world who had refused to accept God's truth. We do not know exactly what "the lie" (v. 11) is that Satan will try to get the world to believe, but part of it will certainly be convincing the world to believe in and worship the Antichrist as God.

What?

We know the *who* of the Antichrist, but we must now turn over the second Clue card to understand the *what*. What does the Antichrist do? The second identifying characteristic focuses on the activities that mark the future leader . . . and two major activities rise to the surface.

The iron fist. The first characteristic activity that helps identify the Antichrist is that he comes wielding an iron fist. In Daniel 7 the prophet describes a vision of four beasts climbing out of the sea. Each beast represents one of the four Gentile powers that would rule over Israel and the Jewish people during the times of the Gentiles. The first was Babylon, the second Medo-Persia, the third Greece, and the fourth Rome. The Roman Empire was, in fact, ruling at the time of Christ's first coming. Though Christ offered the kingdom to Israel, His offer was rejected. The establishment of Israel's kingdom now awaits Christ's second coming. But since Daniel predicted that this fourth empire was to be in power when the Son of Man begins his kingdom, many believe that the Roman Empire must be reconstituted. It must return in some form so that it is in existence at the time of Christ's second coming.

The fourth empire fascinated Daniel. "I wanted to know the true meaning of the fourth beast, which was different from all the others and most terrifying, with its iron teeth and bronze claws—the beast that crushed and devoured its victims and trampled underfoot whatever was left" (Daniel 7:19). Notice carefully the character of this empire. It crushes, devours, and tramples. Just like the Roman Empire in the first century, the final form of this empire—led by the Antichrist—will have the ability to destroy all who dare stand in its way.

Revelation 13 also describes this "beast coming out of the sea" (v. 1). John uses the same picture to help his readers understand that the Roman Empire will again exist in the future. The people in Revelation 13 who worship the Beast ask, "Who is like the beast? Who can make war against him?" (v. 4). No one can stand against or oppose the power of the Antichrist and his empire.

Daniel provides a second characteristic of this iron fist. Not only does the Antichrist crush and devour nations, but he will also persecute God's people. "As I watched, this horn was waging war against the saints and defeating them" (Daniel 7:21). The Antichrist will head a military empire that will conquer the earth. But he will then use that power against those who have put their faith and trust in Jesus Christ. Believing Jews and Gentiles will be singled out. How could this happen? The current war against terrorism illustrates how such an event could take place. Since September 11, the power and might of the United States has been amassed against a group that is united because of its common religious beliefs. The war on terrorism is not a war against Islam, yet all the individuals targeted share that religious system in common. The Antichrist could very well use similar statements to mask the fact that he will be using his power against a group that shares common religious beliefs. And there will be many who will lose their lives at that time.

Daniel 11 reveals a third characteristic about the Antichrist's iron fist. He also honors a god of fortresses. This chapter traces the events of history through the lives of key people. Daniel begins with selected kings from Medo-Persia (v. 2), jumping to Alexander, king of Greece (v. 3), and tracing the division of his empire, focusing especially on the leaders in Egypt and Syria (vv. 4–35). Finally, Daniel transitions to the future (vv. 36–45). As Daniel describes this future world leader, he writes, "He will show no regard for the gods of his fathers or for the one desired by women, nor will he regard any god, but will exalt himself above them all" (v. 37). This is a man who will claim for himself a greatness that exceeds that of any supposed god on earth. Instead of honoring gods, he will "honor a god of fortresses; a god unknown to his fathers he will honor with gold and silver, with precious stones and costly gifts. He will attack the mightiest fortresses with the help of a foreign god and will greatly honor those who acknowledge him" (vv. 38–39). Daniel makes two crucial points. First, he says this leader will "honor a god of fortresses." That is, he will focus on military might. But Daniel also writes that he will conquer others "with the help of a foreign god." That is, he will have supernatural help in achieving his goals. But who is this "foreign god"? It must be Satan. Satan's power, combined with the Antichrist's emphasis on military might, will lead him to victory throughout the world.

The velvet glove. The Antichrist will rule with a fist of iron. But why would anyone follow such a man of warfare and bloodshed, a man bent on world conquest? They will follow him, in part, because his iron fist is, at least initially, masked in a velvet glove. When the Antichrist first appears in Daniel 9:27, he comes as a prince who is making an agreement with Israel. "He will confirm a covenant with many for one 'seven.'" The first appearance of this future world ruler is as a man seeking to bring peace. Since the focus in Daniel 9 is on Israel and Jerusalem, it seems likely that this covenant has something to do with the ongoing search for peace in the Middle East.

From Israel's birth in 1948, through the Six-Day War of 1967, to the Yom Kippur War in 1973, to the invasion of Lebanon, to the current Intifada, Israel has experienced constant struggles with her Arab neighbors. Every recent president of the United States has tried to find a solution that would bring peace to the Middle East—but no one has succeeded. Europe has also been sending envoys to the Middle East to seek an end to the conflict but, thus far, they also have failed. Someday a man will rise to prominence who will broker an agreement that seems to bring peace to the Middle East. It is this agreement that introduces the Antichrist to the world.

The second characteristic of the velvet glove that will mask the iron fist is found in 1 Thessalonians 5. People will accept and follow the Antichrist because he will offer the world peace. In 1 Thessalonians 4 Paul described how God will remove the church from the earth. He then introduced a new topic with his typical Greek phrase *peri de* ("Now concerning"). The new topic introduced by Paul was "the day of the Lord." Paul began by describing the events that would follow the removal of the church from the earth. "Now, brothers, about times and dates we do not need to write to you, for you know very well that the day of the Lord will come like a thief in the night. While people are saying 'Peace and safety,' destruction will come on them suddenly, as labor pains on a pregnant woman, and they will not escape" (1 Thessalonians 5:1–3).

As the end times begin, people will not be looking for destruction. Instead, they will be expecting a time of peace and safety. It will look to them as if "the peace to end all peace" is finally at hand. Such optimism seems to coincide with the introduction of this future ruler. But how can peace and war exist together? How can an individual promise peace by leading the world to war? Once again, events since September 11 provide us with a clear example of how this can happen. Vice President Dick Cheney prepared America for the war against terrorism by reminding us that victory can only come after a period of struggle. "There will be no peaceful coexistence, no negotiations, no summit, no joint communiqué with the terrorists. The struggle can end only with their complete and permanent destruction."

If we want to make the world safe for peace, what do we need to do? We need to destroy those who would oppose it. It takes war to make peace. Charles Krauthammer, writing in *Time* magazine, said, "There are wars of choice, and there are wars of necessity. . . . A war of necessity is a life-or-death struggle in which the safety and security of the homeland are at stake. The war on terrorism is such a war." In short, we are forced to make war so that, ultimately, we can achieve safety and peace and security. You can have war to produce peace.

Don't miss the point here. I am not saying George Bush is the Antichrist or that the United States is the Roman Empire predicted in the books of Daniel and Revelation. What I am saying is that the current conflict has given us an excellent example of how nations can coalesce and how groups can unite behind a strong leader who can lead them into war by promising peace. The future Antichrist will do something very similar.

Some event will trigger the rise of a leader who says to the nations, "It's now time to put an end to the problems plaguing the Middle East and the rest of the world. It's time to bring peace. Follow me, and together we will rid the world of those causing all the problems." An iron fist masked by a velvet glove. War to bring peace. What seemed so paradoxical before now makes perfect sense, because a post–September 11 world now understands how such events can fit together . . . and how they can coalesce so rapidly.

Where?

We know the *who* and the *what*; now we must turn over the final Clue card to discover the *where*. Where is the Antichrist from? Does the Bible help us identify the country or region from which the Antichrist will arise? Actually, four specific passages in God's Word help solve this mystery.

The legs and feet of Daniel 2. In Daniel 2 King Nebuchadnezzar had a dream. In that dream he saw a statue with a head of gold, chest and arms of silver, belly and thighs of bronze, legs of iron, and feet of iron and clay. The dream had significance, and Nebuchadnezzar wanted to know its interpretation. Daniel was finally able to provide Nebuchadnezzar with God's interpretation. "You [Nebuchadnezzar] are that head of gold. After you, another kingdom will rise, inferior to yours" (Daniel 2:38–39a). The head of gold represented Nebuchadnezzar and the Babylonian Empire. The kingdom that followed Babylon was Medo-Persia. The belly and thighs of bronze were interpreted as "a third kingdom" (v. 39). This would be Greece, since Greece followed Medo-Persia in ruling Israel. The fourth empire is one that was to follow Greece, and it will be in existence when the "rock cut out of a mountain, but not by human hands" (a reference to God's kingdom, v. 45) will come to earth, since the rock struck the statue "on its feet of iron and clay" (v. 34). When Jesus came to earth at His first coming, Rome was ruling over the Jewish people. When He returns at His second coming, the same empire must again be in existence. Since Rome was in control at the First Advent, it seems that a revived Roman Empire is the final empire from which the Antichrist will come.

The fourth beast of Daniel 7. The second passage that helps us determine where the Antichrist is from is Daniel 7. In this chapter, four beasts claw their way out of the sea onto land. The first is a lion with wings like an eagle. This seems to picture Babylon. The second beast is a bear raised on one side with three ribs in its teeth. This was a picture of the Medo-Persian Empire, with Persia being the dominant side and the three ribs representing the three empires conquered by Medo-Persia. The third beast is a leopard with four heads that moves rapidly over the earth. The leopard pictures the empire of Greece with Alexander's rapid conquest, and the four heads representing the four generals who carved up the empire following Alexander's death. Finally, a fourth beast came out of the sea. This beast is said to be strong, with teeth like iron and with ten horns. Again, it represents the fourth in a series of empires, and it seems likely that the empire is Rome. The final world ruler (identified as a "little horn") comes from this fourth beast. The Antichrist will arise from the area once ruled by the Roman Empire.

The ruler of Daniel 9. The third passage that can help us determine the Antichrist's location is Daniel 9. The entire prophecy of Daniel 9 was said to be "for your people and your holy city" (v. 24). The first sixty-nine "weeks" of years (483 years) took place from the time a command was given to restore and build Jerusalem until the Messiah. This prophetic period began with the command to rebuild Jerusalem in Nehemiah 2 and ended the day Jesus rode into Jerusalem on Palm Sunday. Daniel then stopped the hands of God's prophetic clock. During this break in the prophetic chronology, Daniel inserted three specific events. First, the Messiah would be "cut off" or killed. This was fulfilled when Jesus died on the cross. Second, Jerusalem would be destroyed by "the people of the ruler who will come." This was fulfilled in A.D. 70 when the Romans destroyed Jerusalem. Third, "war . . . and desolations" (Daniel 9:26) would be poured out on the Jewish people in the intervening time.

But let's go back to the second of these events. Jerusalem was to be destroyed by "the people of the ruler who will come." Since the Romans destroyed Jerusalem, they must be the nation from which this "ruler" comes. In verse 27 Daniel describes the final seven-year period. It starts when "he," the future world leader, makes a covenant. But who is "he"? The nearest antecedent to this pronoun is "the ruler who will come" (v. 26). In effect, Daniel says that the future Antichrist will come from the people who destroyed Jerusalem. Since it was the Roman Empire that destroyed Jerusalem in A.D. 70, this future world ruler must come from an area that was once part of the Roman Empire.

The beast of Revelation 13. The final passage that can help us identify where the Antichrist is from is Revelation 13. The apostle John describes a beast coming up out of the sea, energized by Satan. The beast in Revelation 13 is the same beast described in Daniel 7. In this chapter John provides additional information about the Antichrist and his future kingdom. No one will be able to "make war against him," and he will have power for "forty-two months" (vv. 4–5). By identifying his beast with that of Daniel 7, John seems to be indicating that the fourth empire predicted by Daniel will return to power just before the time of Christ's second coming.

What was the extent of the Roman Empire? A good historical map can be very enlightening. The Roman Empire stretched from Britain on the north down through Europe. It ringed the Mediterranean basin and extended into some parts of the Middle East. Somewhere from within that geographical region is the place from which the Antichrist will rise to rule the world.

In Summary

The three Clue cards are now spread out, faceup, on the playing board. By looking at them together, a clear picture of the future Antichrist emerges.

- The Antichrist will be a great worldwide deceiver who will rise to power through the work of Satan.
- The Antichrist will be a man of war who will come to power promising peace, especially peace in the Middle East.
- The Antichrist will emerge from the area once ruled by the Roman Empire.

WHEN WILL THESE THINGS BE?

We do not know the exact time when the Antichrist will arise because we don't know when the end times will begin. But if the last days are close, could the Antichrist be alive today? Two answers seem to emerge from God's Word.

The Antichrist Will Arise According to God's Timetable

The Bible states that the Antichrist's appearance is being held back by God's omnipotence until the proper time. As stated earlier, Paul made this very clear in his letter to the Thessalonians. "And now you know what is holding him back, so that he may be revealed at the proper time. For the secret power of lawlessness is already at work; but the one who now holds it back will continue to do so till he is taken out of the way. And then the lawless one will be revealed" (2 Thessalonians 2:6–8). We don't know when the Antichrist will arise, but it will happen in God's perfect time. When God has the world stage completely set and is ready to begin His end-time drama, then the Antichrist will be revealed. Only God knows when that time will come.

Potential Antichrists Have Always Existed

Since Satan is not omniscient, he does not know when God will begin His end-time program. As a result, Satan has always had to have a potential candidate waiting on the sideline who could step in to fill the role. Perhaps this is what the apostle John meant when he wrote, "Dear children, this is the last hour; and as you have heard that the antichrist is coming, even now many antichrists have come" (1 John 2:18). John believed that the end times were close at hand. He didn't know when they would begin, but he assumed the time was close. John had also taught that a future Antichrist would appear in the end times.

But then John reminded his readers that "even now

many antichrists have come." Evidently, there have been "wanna-be" antichrists throughout history. But this should come as no surprise. Satan must have had potential anti-christs ready throughout history because he never knew when God would remove His church from this earth and begin the final period of trouble that ends with the second coming of Christ.

SO WHAT?

God never revealed the future merely to fill our heads with knowledge. God has always intended prophecy to have a practical application to the here and now. So this chapter needs to end by asking a key question: So what? What difference does this truth make in our lives? First, knowing what the Bible says about this future leader should give us *confidence* that God is in control. God may end your life here on earth and take you to heaven, but you can be sure that you will never die and go there by accident. You will pass from this life into eternity only when God decides that the time has come. He is in control.

Second, knowing what the Bible says about this future Antichrist can give us *hope*. Even as we watch the world seeming to slide toward the end times, we are reminded that God is in control and that His program for the church ends before His final seven-year program for Israel resumes. Today's headlines simply mean that our redemption is nearer today than it has ever been . . . and that gives us hope.

Third, knowing about the program for the future Anti-christ should spur us on to *holiness*. The destruction he will bring on this earth is a reminder that the world isn't all there is to life. Our true home is in eternity, not here on earth. Most Americans watched in horrified amazement as the World Trade Centers tumbled down. The towers had seemed so permanent, but they were not. Those images, combined with the truth of God's Word, should spur us on to remember what really is permanent and what is only temporary in our lives.

My favorite gospel song is "It Is Well with My Soul." The words were written by a Chicagoan named Horatio Spafford. He was a lawyer who did quite well until the Great Chicago Fire roared through the city. This disaster was Chicago's version of the World Trade Center collapse, though it was caused by natural forces, not terrorists. The fire burned Spafford's law offices to the ground. Over the next two years, most of Spafford's other investments collapsed. His personal wealth diminished greatly during this time.

Spafford had promised to take his family to Europe. Though he was still trying to salvage some of his investments, he felt that he needed to send his wife and daughters on ahead. The day their ship sailed from New York City, the deal he was working on fell through. He could have traveled with them, though he had no way of knowing it at the time. The *Ville du Harve,* the ship on which his family was sailing, was struck by another ship in the Atlantic Ocean; and it sank in twelve minutes. Mrs. Spafford rushed her daughters up on deck; but when the ship slipped under the waves, the children were pulled from her arms and drowned. Mrs. Spafford lost consciousness, only to awaken in a small lifeboat. She was one of the few who were rescued from the cold waters. When the rescue ship reached Europe, she sent a cable to her husband that described the tragedy in two stark words: SAVED ALONE.

Compare your problems to those that pounded against the life of Horatio Spafford. He was struggling financially, but those struggles paled in comparison to the sense of loss he felt when he received the sad news of his children's deaths. Spafford went immediately to New York City and boarded a ship to go to be with his wife. One night on the ship, the captain came to him to tell him that they were very near the spot where the *Ville du Harve* had gone down. How would you have responded to this time of trouble if it had been you? Horatio Spafford's reaction was truly amazing . . . and has been preserved for us in two ways.

The first way we know Horatio Spafford's reaction is through a letter he wrote to his sister, Rachel, describing his feelings.

> On Thursday last we passed over the spot where [the ship] went down, in mid-ocean, the water three miles deep. But I do not think of our dear ones there. They are safe, folded, the dear lambs, and there, before very long, shall we be too. In the meantime, thanks to God, we have an opportunity to serve and praise Him for His love and mercy to us and ours. "I will praise Him while I have my being." May we each one arise, leave all, and follow Him.

As I read those words, I'm impressed with his great faith. The second way we know Horatio Spafford's reaction is through a poem he wrote during this time. I have a lithograph of that poem on my office wall. The words were later set to music, and that is my favorite gospel song. The poem was written on a borrowed piece of stationery from the Brevoort House hotel that once stood on Clark Street between Madison and LaSalle in downtown Chicago. Unfortunately, the building no longer exists. Spafford took that piece of stationery and folded it to keep in his coat pocket. Evidently, he kept pulling it out as he wrote his poem, because the creases are clearly visible on the original, on display at the American Colony Hotel in Jerusalem, and on the lithograph. The words to the first stanza appear in our hymnbooks almost exactly as he first penned them.

When peace like a river, attendeth my way,
When sorrows like sea billows roll;
Whatever my lot, Thou hast taught me to say,
"It is well, it is well with my soul."

I marvel at these great words, but how could Horatio Spafford possess that kind of confidence, faith, and hope? I didn't have an answer until I looked very carefully at the last verse. That is the verse Spafford labored over the most. There are several places on that piece of old hotel stationery where he scratched out his first words and wrote in others. In some places entire lines were replaced. It's as though he agonized over the last stanza to make sure he could get it just right. And what words did Spafford finally decide on for that final stanza?

And Lord, haste the day when the faith shall be sight,
The clouds be rolled back as a scroll,
The trump shall resound and the Lord shall descend,
"Even so"—it is well with my soul.

What kept Spafford on track spiritually? Every line in the final stanza shows that his focus was on the future. He knew that God was in control and that someday God would make things right. A time would come when Spafford would again see his children in heaven. His questions would be answered. God would wipe the tears from his eyes. His hope in the future gave him stability to live in the present. In that last stanza, Spafford looked forward to the day when Jesus would come to take him to heaven.

But I always puzzled over the last line. Spafford ended

with the somewhat obscure phrase, "'Even so'—it is well with my soul." When I first read it, it was as though Spafford was saying, "Jesus is coming back and 'even so,' that's OK." But then I realized what I had missed for so long. Look carefully at the last line. When Spafford had this line just the way he wanted, he had placed the words *even so* in quotation marks with a dash following. Throughout the whole last stanza, Spafford was quoting from, or alluding to, specific passages of Scripture that focus on Christ's return. When he wrote "'Even so'—" he was still quoting Scripture, and he expected his readers to know the verse . . . and to complete it. The verse he started to quote is the next-to-the-last verse in the book of Revelation. In the King James Version, which Spafford was using, Jesus said, "Surely I come quickly," And the apostle John's response was "Amen. Even so, come, Lord Jesus." Spafford wanted his readers to finish the verse . . . to pray back to God their confidence in His promise to return, to take His children to heaven, to complete His program for the ages. Knowing this truth allowed Spafford to say with confidence, "It is well with my soul."

There is an Antichrist. He is going to come . . . and God revealed all this in advance to assure us that He is in control. The Antichrist will come after the church is raptured to heaven. Many antichrists have come, and the church has experienced Satan's fiery trials here on earth. But through it all, those who understand God's program for the future breathe back to God, "Amen. Even so, come, Lord Jesus." And we know that it is—and will remain forever—well with our souls.

2 GROUND ZERO

Dr. Michael Rydelnik

September 11, 2001. The World Trade Center aflame, a second plane crashing into the towers, massive structures crumbling to the ground. Thousands dead while rescue workers vanish into smoke and debris. These images ever remain before our eyes. "Ground Zero" will be forever imprinted on our mind's eye: a burning, smoking ruin where monumental skyscrapers of concrete and steel once stood. When we think of "Ground Zero," we remember the rubble and the rescue workers, the firemen and police officers of New York City. These days we are focusing on the devastation left by the terrorist attack, but in the future there will be a different "Ground Zero."

The "Ground Zero" of tomorrow is not in New York City but in the land of Israel, and the city of Jerusalem, according to biblical prophecy. The Bible reveals there will be vast and devastating future events that will occur on that narrow strip of land, which is only about the size of New Jersey.

This is where the Lord's deliverance will come. The focus of this chapter is the "Ground Zero" of the future: the centrality of Israel in Bible prophecy. In it, we will examine four crucial experiences that will mark Israel as "Ground Zero."

FALSE PEACE

The attempts to establish peace in the Middle East did not begin recently; there have been numerous attempts to broker peace in the past. One of the first attempts, in 1918, was between Emir Feisal, the son of the sherif of Mecca and Medina, and Chaim Weizmann, the leader of world Zionism, who later became the first president of Israel. They came to an agreement immediately after World War I. However, the plan was never adopted because of other designs that the French and British had on the Middle East. Since the establishment of the State of Israel in 1948, there have been repeated attempts to establish peace between the Arabs and Israel. Operating under the auspices of the League of Nations, and, later, the United Nations, the British, various European states, the former Soviet Union, and the United States, at different times and in different ways, have all tried to establish a comprehensive peace. But all have failed.

In the last forty years, the United States government has been at the forefront of peace efforts. Though our country did broker peace treaties between Israel and her two neighbors, Egypt and Jordan, these have not erased their past hostility. Indeed, these nations share what they call "a cold peace." Even the Oslo accords, which gave so much hope for peace between Israel and the Palestinians, have crashed with the onslaught of the second Palestinian Intifada. We can only wonder, Will there ever be a true and lasting peace in this troubled region of the world?

The Scriptures do promise that there will be peace, but

only a temporary one. In 1 Thessalonians 5:2–3, the apostle Paul wrote that the Day of the Lord will arrive as suddenly and unexpectedly as labor pains on a pregnant woman. People will think that peace has finally come, so they will be saying "peace and safety." Then when the Day of the Lord arrives, with destruction and the worst wars in history, people will be astounded and taken by surprise. The Day of the Lord will arrive without warning in the midst of a time the world thought would bring peace.

The ancient Jewish prophet Daniel foretold the source of this false peace. In Daniel 9:27 the prophet predicted that a future false messiah—the Antichrist—will make a covenant with the nation of Israel: "He will confirm a covenant with many." The one who makes this covenant is the future false messiah, called in verse 26 "the ruler who will come." He will make a covenant with "many," referring either to the leadership of Israel or to the whole nation viewed collectively. This ruler will offer peace, though in reality he will be a man of war. With political skill and persuasive speech, he will use all his satanic and supernatural guile to bring a false sense of peace to Israel. With the signing of this covenant of peace between Israel and the Antichrist, the world will be saying "peace and safety." At that time, the Day of the Lord will come.

Imagine how excited people will be with the establishment of peace in the Middle East. I think back to September 13, 1993, the day the Oslo accords were signed by Yitzhak Rabin and Yasser Arafat on the White House lawn. It was unbelievable when Israel and the PLO formally entered into a pact of mutual recognition. Before this, I had always believed that there would be perpetual war between Israel and the Palestinians. That was distressing because my family lives in Israel. All my cousins went into the military when they turned eighteen. All of them fought in wars and risked their lives doing reserve duty in the administered territories. War was a reality and an expectation for all of us.

As hard as it was for me to believe that the violence would come to an end, there was Yitzhak Rabin shaking hands with Yasser Arafat after they signed the Oslo agreement of principles. Israel and the Palestinians agreed that there would be no more war or violence. They said they would settle all their differences at the peace table by negotiations and discussions. Not only did the majority of Israelis and Palestinians rejoice, so did the rest of the world.

By September 2000, all the great hopes of the Oslo accords came crashing apart with a renewed Palestinian uprising. Almost daily, the news media contains reports on suicide bombers killing Israelis at pizza parlors and cafes, in drive-by shootings, and on pitched battles between Palestinians and Israeli troops. The front pages show how fragile peace really is . . . and how rapidly it can end.

The disappointing collapse of the Oslo accords and the renewed violence in the Middle East is a harbinger of what the future holds. The future false messiah will establish peace for Israel. But it will not be a lasting and true peace. Instead it will be temporary and false. The nation of Israel will enter into this accord thinking that peace has arrived. Daniel 9:27 says that after three-and-a-half years the Antichrist will break his covenant, and the peace will be shattered. So the first phase of Israel as "Ground Zero" in biblical prophecy is that it will be the place where peace, albeit a false one, will be established.

FUTURE PERSECUTION

The second way that Israel will be the "Ground Zero" of future events is that the nation will experience future persecution. The prophet Jeremiah announced that Israel's future will include a day of tribulation and trouble. "How awful that day will be! None will be like it. It will be a time of trouble for Jacob, but he will be saved out of it" (Jeremiah 30:7). This "time of trouble" will begin after the Antichrist breaks the peace treaty he has made with Israel.

The Details of the Persecution

Zechariah 14 provides several clear details of Israel's coming distress. This passage is a snapshot of the Day of the Lord (a time many Bible teachers call the Tribulation period). Zechariah began by announcing, "A day of the LORD is coming when your plunder will be divided among you. I will gather all the nations to Jerusalem to fight against it" (Zechariah 14:1–2). The first detail that Zechariah gives is the gathering of all the nations against Jerusalem. Where do they come from? They come from nations throughout the earth, and they will gather in northern Israel, in the Jezreel Valley near Mount Megiddo, to begin the campaign of Armageddon (Revelation 16:14–16). Ultimately, they will march to Jerusalem and surround the city. All the nations of the earth will be united in their opposition to Israel and the Jewish people. The nations will besiege Jerusalem . . . and there will seem to be no escape for the people of Israel.

You may wonder if it is really possible for all the nations of the world to be against Israel. How many allies do you think Israel has today? The United States stands alone among the major nations of the world as Israel's steadfast ally. And even now there are elements within our nation who argue that it would be better for us if we did not support the State of Israel. They suggest that it might be to our advantage to abandon Israel so that we would be in a better position to maintain our coalition of nations against terrorism.

Perhaps you remember that, just one week before the terrorist attack of September 11, the United Nations held a conference on racism in Durban, South Africa. The nations of the world gathered together . . . and their purpose was to unite to fight racism. But what did they do? Instead of fighting racism, they engaged in it. The conference unleashed some of the most venomous anti-Semitism since the Nazi era. The Non-Governmental Organization (NGO) participants approved a document that maliciously indicted Israel as a "racist, apartheid state," falsely accusing Israel of genocide and ethnic cleansing.

The conference refused to revoke the credentials of a group distributing pamphlets with grotesque caricatures of hook-nosed Jews, depicted as Nazis, spearing Palestinian children, with blood dripping from their fangs. A placard at the conference said, "Hitler should have finished the job." Some present at the conference distributed a flyer with a picture of Hitler and asked, "What if Hitler had won? There would be no Israel and no Palestinian bloodshed." The anti-Semitism was so bad that Secretary of State Colin Powell, leader of the U.S. delegation, left in protest, along with all the U.S. representatives.

If the Non-Governmental Organization participants could vote that Zionism (the belief that there should be a Jewish state in the historic homeland of Israel) is racist, why should we be surprised to see the nations gathered against Jerusalem at some point in the future? Reports in the daily press make it easy to believe Zechariah's prediction of the nations gathering against Jerusalem. Anti-Semitism has been one of the great hatreds of all time; therefore, the nations, motivated by their hatred of the Jewish people, will gather against Jerusalem. If there is one comfort, it is that the Lord says, "I will gather all the nations" (Zechariah 14:2). Although the nations are driven by hatred, they still act under the sovereign plan of God to accomplish His purposes. And His hand will limit them as He gathers them to achieve His ends.

A second detail that Zechariah gives is that there will be a devastation of Jerusalem. "The city will be captured, the houses ransacked, and the women raped. Half of the city will go into exile, but the rest of the people will not be taken from the city" (14:2). This snapshot of the Day of the Lord describes houses being plundered, women being ravaged, half the city going into exile, and others remaining under siege, suffering from a lack of food and water. Zechariah paints a horrible picture of what it will be like in Jerusalem. It will be a devastating time for the Jewish people living in Jerusalem—"Ground Zero" in its most horrific form.

God's Purpose for the Persecution

Having looked at the details of Israel's distress, it is important to understand God's purposes in allowing Israel's devastation. There are two main purposes God has in permitting this future persecution of the Jewish people. The first purpose is to discipline the nation. After identifying Jacob's future time of trouble God promised, "'I am with you and will save you,' declares the LORD. 'Though I completely destroy all the nations among which I scatter you, I will not completely destroy you. *I will discipline you* but only with justice'" (Jeremiah 30:11, italics added). Although the nation of Israel has not been rejected by God (Romans 11:1), for the most part it has rejected God's Messiah, Jesus. Certainly there are Jewish people who believe Jesus is the Jewish Messiah (I am one of them!); but the vast majority do not. God will use the devastation of Jerusalem to discipline the nation so that it will turn to the Messiah Jesus in faith.

God's second purpose in allowing the devastation of Jerusalem is to purge Israel of rebels. In a context describing the Tribulation period God promises, "I will take note of you [Israel] as you pass under my rod, and I will bring you into the bond of the covenant. I will *purge you of those who revolt and rebel* against me" (Ezekiel 20:37–38, italics added). God will make Israel pass "under my rod," which is a figure for discipline. Then God promises to "purge" the nation of its rebels. It is clear that God's purpose is redemptive, not punitive. He wants to cleanse Israel and to bring her into the bond of the covenant.

God will allow the devastation of Jerusalem to bring Israel to faith in her true Messiah, the only hope of salvation. God loves His people Israel. Scripture calls Israel God's son. And as a result of His love, God will discipline the nation and purge it of rebels. These are God's purposes for allowing this terrible time of distress. After Israel experiences a time of false peace followed by terrible persecution, there will be yet another way in which Israel will be "Ground Zero" for future events.

FULL PARDON

A third way that Israel will be the "Ground Zero" of Bible prophecy is that the nation will experience full pardon. How does that happen? God explained the process. "And I will pour out on the house of David and the inhabitants of Jerusalem a spirit of grace and supplication. They will look on me, the one they have pierced, and they will mourn for him as one mourns for an only child, and grieve bitterly for him as one grieves for a firstborn son" (Zechariah 12:10). Once again, the setting is the future Tribulation period. The nations have gathered against Israel, and Israel is facing a terrible time of devastation and difficulty. They will then ask, "Why has all this horror happened to us? To whom can we turn for deliverance?" And God will respond by pouring out His Spirit "on the house of David and the inhabitants of Jerusalem." As God pours out His Spirit, Israel nationally will look to their pierced Messiah, Jesus, in faith. The nation as a whole, at that point in time, will finally recognize that Jesus is the Promised One, and they will acknowledge Him as their Messiah and Lord.

Because Zechariah says that Israel will "look on me, the

one they have pierced," many have misused this verse to say the Bible teaches that the Jewish people bear unique guilt for the death of Jesus. Although this is a reference to the crucifixion of the Messiah, it is not accusing Israel of unique responsibility for His death. In Acts 4:27–28, the early church prayed to God after Peter and John reported on the response to their message. In the prayer, the believers clearly state that many people participated in the crucifixion, including Herod Antipas, Pontius Pilate, and the Roman soldiers. It was a conspiracy of guilt. Indeed, Isaiah 53:5 says, "he was pierced for our transgressions." The apostle Paul agreed in Romans 5:6 when he wrote that "Christ died for the ungodly." Who is responsible for the death of Jesus? We *all* are . . . because He died to pay the penalty for our sin.

Nevertheless, Zechariah 12:10 says that in the future the Jewish nation will recognize that Jesus is the One who was pierced by their ancestors. When the Jewish people realize that Jesus is the Messiah, they will repent with the intense mourning of regret for having rejected Him in the past. There will be great weeping, "as one mourns for an only child." Think of David's lamentation for Absalom, his rebellious child, who was one of several sons (2 Samuel 18:33). Imagine how one would mourn for an only son. Israel will grieve and mourn for the many years of rejecting their Messiah, Jesus, the Son of God. Not only will Israel's repentance be intense; it will also be national. Just as in the past the leaders of Israel rejected the Messiah Jesus with the nation following their lead, so also in the future when the leadership of Israel believes in Jesus, the nation will follow their lead. In that day, the entire nation will turn in faith to Jesus and will be delivered by Him.

As a result of Israel's turning in faith to Jesus the Messiah, the nation will be cleansed from sin. Zechariah described the results of that future day of repentance. "On that day a fountain will be opened to the house of David and the inhabitants of Jerusalem, to cleanse them from sin and impurity" (Zechariah 13:1). When the nation looks to Jesus in faith and repentance, God will "cleanse them from sin" by providing His pardon and forgiveness. All the sin of rebellion and rejection will be removed from the nation at that time. This is the event Paul had in mind when he wrote, "And so all Israel will be saved" (Romans 11:26). He was not referring to all Jewish people for all time. Rather, he was referring to those Jewish people living at the return of Jesus the Messiah. The nation will then be cleansed from all its sin. What a picture! The Messiah will return to cleanse His people from all their sin, and Israel will be completely forgiven.

Israel's repentance and cleansing from sin are essential to the Messiah's return. Many people do not realize that the nation of Israel holds the key to the second coming of Christ. The words of Jesus at His first coming point to the pivotal role Israel plays in His second coming. "O Jerusalem, Jerusalem . . . how often I have longed to gather your children together, as a hen gathers her chicks under her wings, but you were not willing. Look, your house is left to you desolate. For I tell you, you will not see me again until you say, 'Blessed is he who comes in the name of the Lord'" (Matthew 23:37–39).

The Messiah Himself announced that He will not return until Israel says, *"Baruch ha-ba-a bashem Adoni"* ("Blessed is he who comes in the name of the Lord"). This is the traditional Hebrew phrase for greeting and welcome. Therefore, the Messiah Jesus told Israel that He will return only when they welcome Him. That will only happen when, in fulfillment of Zechariah 12:10 and 13:1, Israel turns in faith to Messiah Jesus to be cleansed from sin. When Israel welcomes Jesus as their Messiah, He will return.

FINAL PROTECTION

The fourth aspect of Israel being "Ground Zero" in Bible prophecy is that she will be in the center of God's protection. When the nations besiege and devastate Israel, the nation as a whole will turn to its Messiah and find forgiveness from Him. Then God will deliver Israel both spiritually and physically. At that time God will provide Israel with final protection from all its enemies. In Zechariah 14 the prophet described five ways the Lord will protect and defend Israel.

God Will Rescue the Jewish People in Jerusalem
Zechariah described God's response to the attack on His people.

> Then the LORD will go out and fight against those nations, as he fights in the day of battle. On that day his feet will stand on the Mount of Olives, east of Jerusalem, and the Mount of Olives will be split in two from east to west, forming a great valley, with half of the mountain moving north and half moving south. You will flee by my mountain valley, for it will extend to Azel. You will flee as you fled from the earthquake in the days of Uzziah king of Judah. (Zechariah 14:3–5)

Zechariah had earlier described the nations besieging and devastating Jerusalem. How will the Jewish people escape? When the Messiah returns, He will arrive at the Mount of Olives, just as was promised in Acts 1:11. There the angel told the disciples who had just observed Jesus' ascension that He would return in just the same way that He ascended. Since He ascended from the Mount of Olives, He will return to the Mount of Olives. When He returns, "his feet will stand on the Mount of Olives," and the mount will be split in half, providing the pathway of escape for the besieged people of Jerusalem.

There are some who believe there is a geological fault line running through the Mount of Olives that helps prove this prophecy is plausible. However, be assured that Jesus does not need a geological fault line. When the Messiah returns to the Mount of Olives, His feet will stand on the mountain; and it will part . . . with or without a fault line! That is how He will provide a way of escape. He will fight *for* His people Israel and *against* the nations that have gathered to destroy Israel. The phrase "the LORD will go out and fight" is a technical expression that was used of a warrior-king going out to battle. God will not only provide a way of escape for His people, but He will also be their warrior-king who will deliver them from their enemies.

God Will Renovate the Geography of Israel and Jerusalem

God will entirely change the physical appearance of Israel and Jerusalem.

> On that day there will be no light, no cold or frost. It will
> be a unique day, without daytime or nighttime—a day
> known to the LORD. When evening comes, there will be light.
> On that day living water will flow out from Jerusalem, half to
> the eastern sea and half to the western sea, in summer and in
> winter. The LORD will be king over the whole earth. On that
> day there will be one LORD, and his name the only name. The
> whole land, from Geba to Rimmon, south of Jerusalem, will
> become like the Arabah. But Jerusalem will be raised up and
> remain in its place, from the Benjamin Gate to the site of the
> First Gate, to the Corner Gate, and from the Tower of
> Hananel to the royal winepresses. It will be inhabited; never
> again will it be destroyed. Jerusalem will be secure.
> (Zechariah 14:6–11)

God will renovate both Israel and the city of Jerusalem,

and He will even change the way the days operate. There will be a new river of living water flowing out both to the Mediterranean Sea and to the Dead Sea. It will flow year-round, relieving the cycle of drought and water shortage in the Middle East. Over the past few years, Israel experienced its worst drought in many decades. However, in the future the Lord will relieve the problem of drought forever.

Zechariah also described physical changes to Jerusalem. The land surrounding the city will be level; but Jerusalem will be raised up, making it more prominent than any other city. God will do this because Jerusalem will not just be the capital of Israel, as it is now. One day Jerusalem will be the capital of the whole world, with the Messiah seated on His throne there, reigning over the whole earth from Jerusalem.

One of the many political disputes of our day pertains to the capital of Israel. Both Israelis and Palestinians claim Jerusalem as their capital. As a result, the United States has maintained its Israeli embassy in the city of Tel Aviv. During every presidential election the candidates, in a calculated attempt to get the Jewish vote, promise to move the embassy to Jerusalem. Once elected, these politicians have always said, "Well, not right now." In the future God will settle the question of sovereignty over Jerusalem once and for all. He will do that by placing the city under the authority of the Messianic King of Israel who will reign over Israel and the world. The nations will have no choice regarding the location of their embassies. They will have to come to Jerusalem because that is where the King Messiah will reign. Jerusalem will be elevated as capital of both Israel and the world.

God Will Judge the Oppressors of Jerusalem

Zechariah described God's judgment on the enemies of Israel. "This is the plague with which the LORD will strike all the nations that fought against Jerusalem: Their flesh will rot while they are still standing on their feet, their eyes will rot in their sockets, and their tongues will rot in their mouths" (14:12). You may remember the scene in the movie *Raiders of the Lost Ark,* when the Nazis peered into the ark of the covenant, resulting in their skin melting off their faces. Though entirely fictitious, it was probably a good visualization of the plague God will bring on Israel's enemies!

God will also protect Israel by causing a panic among the attackers of Jerusalem. "On that day men will be stricken by the LORD with great panic. Each man will seize the hand of another, and they will attack each other. Judah too will fight at Jerusalem" (vv. 13–14). God gives Israel a great victory and allows it to plunder the wealth of the nations that attacked it. Israel will collect "great quantities of gold and silver and clothing" (v. 14).

God will judge the nations who have attacked Jerusalem by pouring out on them plague, panic, and plundering. This judgment is in fulfillment of the Abrahamic covenant, which promises that God will bless those who bless Israel and curse those who curse her (Genesis 12:3). In Zechariah 14:2, the nations come against Jerusalem to ransack and plunder. Now the very same curse will fall on them.

Throughout history, when any nation (and there have been many!) gathered to destroy or harm the Jewish people, God would rise up to defend His people. God cursed Pharaoh for enslaving and attempting to destroy Israel. As a result of God's faithfulness in protecting the Jewish people, Passover is still celebrated to this day. The book of Esther also records how Haman tried to annihilate the Jewish people. But today Jewish people celebrate God's defeat of Haman with the Festival of Purim. A friend of mine says that every time the Gentiles try to destroy the Jews, Israel gets another holiday!

Though Zechariah is speaking about events in the future, it would also be wise to consider our own attitudes toward the Jewish people today. Consider the Jewish people you know, whether a neighbor, coworker, schoolmate, or business associate. Perhaps your doctor or lawyer is Jewish. What is your perspective on the Jewish people? Hopefully, if you are reading this, you have rejected those attitudes of hatred and resentment that have fueled anti-Semitism. Followers of the Jewish Messiah should be noted for their love of His people, for they are the apple of God's eye.

God Will Require Universal Worship in Jerusalem

After describing God's great victory, Zechariah predicted that the warriors will become worshipers who will come to Jerusalem to celebrate a great Jewish holiday.

> The survivors from all the nations that have attacked Jerusalem will go up year after year to worship the King, the LORD Almighty, and to celebrate the Feast of Tabernacles. If any of the peoples of the earth do not go up to Jerusalem to worship the King, the LORD Almighty, they will have no rain. If the Egyptian people do not go up and take part, they will have no rain. The LORD will bring on them the plague he inflicts on the nations that do not go up to celebrate the Feast of Tabernacles. This will be the punishment of Egypt and the punishment of all the nations that do not go up to celebrate the Feast of Tabernacles. (Zechariah 14:16–19)

Zechariah is saying that during the messianic kingdom, God will require the nations to worship Him at the Festival of Sukkoth (Tabernacles).

Why Sukkoth? The most likely explanation is that Sukkoth is a holy day that looked forward to the messianic kingdom, when the Messiah will dwell (tabernacle) with His people. In the future messianic kingdom, the Messiah will be physically dwelling on earth, reigning from Jerusalem. Therefore, all the nations in the kingdom will join Israel in

celebrating God's presence during the festival that anticipated His kingdom. Even Egypt will have to celebrate
Sukkoth. If the nation does not come to worship, it will
experience drought. In fact, if any nation refuses to join the
celebration, it will be punished. In the future, the whole
world will worship the God of Israel.

God Will Bring About Total Holiness

The prophet Zechariah also predicted that God's future
kingdom would be a time of holiness.

> On that day HOLY TO THE LORD will be inscribed on the
> bells of the horses, and the cooking pots in the LORD's house
> will be like the sacred bowls in front of the altar. Every pot in
> Jerusalem and Judah will be holy to the LORD Almighty, and
> all who come to sacrifice will take some of the pots and cook
> in them. And on that day there will no longer be a Canaanite
> in the house of the LORD Almighty. (Zechariah 14:20–21)

In these verses, God is promising that in the messianic
kingdom there will no longer be any division between the
sacred and the profane. Even the horses and the cooking
pots will be "holy," meaning they will be "set apart" to the
Lord. Everything about the city will be consecrated to God.
Zechariah also announced that there will no longer be a
"Canaanite." He is likely referring to all unclean people
rather than to one specific group of people. Why will there
be no unclean people in Jerusalem? Because Israel and all
the nations will have been cleansed, and they will enter
Jerusalem as a holy people coming to worship God.

CONCLUSION

Sometimes events in the news can lead us to despair.
When terrorists fly planes into buildings, killing thousands,

or suicide bombers kill teenagers at birthday parties and pizza parlors, we might begin to doubt God's promise that He will indeed set the world aright in His kingdom. Evil circumstances today can sometimes lead us to doubt God's certain promises for the future. But God has already assured us that His victory is secure.

As a child I loved to watch the old *Superman* television show. I watched every episode. When my son was a young boy, he also fell in love with the show, then appearing on a station that specialized in "classic" old television programs. He and I would sit and watch the reruns together. It seemed that in every other episode some bad guy would try to use kryptonite to endanger Superman's life. When my young son would see this, he would get distressed and anxious. I would then assure him that everything would turn out well. "How do you know, Dad?" he would ask in a worried voice. My answer was that I had seen this episode before, so I knew how it would end. Superman would survive . . . and would win! Nevertheless, my son would worry, even though an authoritative source (his very own dad!) had assured him of the end of the story. He would look at the tough circumstances Superman faced instead of the true certainty of how the show would end.

We make the same mistake when we look at the circumstances of September 11, or anthrax scares, or the battles that rage in Israel. The world looks bleak today and, according to the Scriptures, it will look even bleaker for Israel in that future Day of the Lord. We could become anxious if we only looked at circumstances, but we know how the show will end. An authoritative and true source (the Bible) has told us how history will unfold. In the end, the Messiah Jesus will return, defend His people, and establish His righteous kingdom. Even as we watch events unfolding at "Ground Zero," we can have hope as long as we remain focused on the good certainties of God's Word rather than the evil circumstances of our times.

3 THE FUTURE OF ISLAMIC FUNDAMENTALISM

Dr. Samuel Naaman

The tragic events of September 11 forced most Americans to admit that they knew very little about Islam . . . the third monotheistic religion to arise in the Middle East. Suddenly, the beliefs and practices of Islam were reported—and debated—on television news programs and talk shows. Books on Islam appeared on store shelves, and the Qur'an (which some might recognize by the older English spelling Koran) became a top-selling book.

The events of September 11 also forced the government of the United States to walk a careful—though often convoluted—path in its battle with the Al Qaeda terrorist organization. Government officials have tried to avoid framing the conflict in religious terms, even though all the terrorist groups connected with Al Qaeda share one element in common . . . Islamic fundamentalism. But the United States sought to separate the terrorists from their religious convictions because the coalition it built included Islamic nations.

The need to fight terrorism without offending Islamic states even forced America to make some major changes in its foreign policy.

President Musharraf, the leader of Pakistan, was considered by the United States to be little more than a dictator on September 10. By September 12 he had become an ally and a partner with the United States in our war against terrorism. Since September 11 the United States has lifted sanctions it had previously imposed on Sudan, Pakistan, and India. What a difference a day makes!

But what do the events of September 11 have in common with Islam . . . and with a 2,500-year-old prophecy found in the book of Ezekiel? To understand the significance, one must first understand Islam. How did Islam begin, and what does it believe?

THE REALITY OF ISLAM

Islam's Beginning

Muhammad was born in Saudi Arabia, and that is the land from which Islam emerged. At first, Muhammad expected his teaching to be accepted by both Jews and Christians. Initially, the direction of prayer, or *kiblah,* for Muslims was Jerusalem. But when the Jews refused to accept Muhammad as a prophet, the direction of prayer changed from Jerusalem to Mecca. The Muslims also appropriated the site of Israel's temple into their religious tradition. The exposed rock on which the ark of the covenant once rested in Solomon's temple became the site on which they built the Dome of the Rock. In Islamic teaching, this was the spot from which Muhammad ascended to heaven on his night journey.

Islam also incorporated some elements of Christianity into its beliefs. For example, Muslims believe that Jesus will return to Jerusalem. "By Him in Whose Hands my soul is, son of Mary [i.e., Jesus] will shortly descend amongst you [Muslims] as a just ruler and will break the cross and kill the pig and abolish the *Jizya* [a tax taken from the non-Muslims, who are under the protection of the Muslim government]. Then there will be abundance of money and nobody will accept charitable gifts" (Sahih Bukhari [34.104.425]).

Islam's Beliefs

Surrender to God. The word *Islam* is music to the soul of the Muslim. It suggests everything that a Muslim holds dear to life. The term itself comes from the word *salama,* which means "to surrender" or "to be at peace." As a result, many believe that Islam is chiefly a religion of peace. But first of all, Islam is a religion of surrender. Muslims believe that as humans surrender to God and His will they ultimately obtain peace and satisfaction.

Five pillars of Islam. The five pillars of Islam are the main expression of this surrender to Allah. These are (a) confession that Allah alone is God and that Muhammad is His prophet; (b) set periods of prayer each day; (c) fasting during the month of Ramadan; (d) almsgiving; and (e) embarking on a pilgrimage to Mecca once during one's lifetime. These are the daily life practices of a Muslim, and obedience to them is necessary for living a life in complete surrender to God. Through the Qur'an God's will is clearly revealed, and the task of every human in this world is to submit to that revelation.

Uniqueness of God. Central to Islam is the belief that there is one God who is alone God. He can have no partners, and no one is equal to Him. The greatest blasphemy, and most unforgivable sin, is to assign partners to God or to worship another as equal to Him. Only He is all-powerful and all-wise. This is why Muslims struggle with the truth that Jesus is God's Son. While Muslims do believe that God has other attributes such as love and compassion, they believe God's power and eminence are most important.

Islam's worldwide community. From Juddah, Saudi Arabia, to Jacksonville, Florida; from Dhaka, Bangladesh, to Detroit, Michigan; from Jakarta, Indonesia, to Joliet, Illinois; from Lahore, Pakistan, to Los Angeles, California . . . all Muslims are part of the Muslim world. The Muslim community is, in one sense, a mother to all Muslims. The community gives to the individual members a sense of fellowship and security. The whole Muslim community is one body and feels all things in common. The profile of the Muslim community reveals something interesting. The majority of the world's Muslims live beyond the Middle East and are not of Arab descent. The world of Islam is truly multicultural!

Islam's struggle against the rest of the world. Islam makes a major distinction between the "House of Islam" and the "House of War." All humanity belongs either to one house or to the other. There are no geographical or political boundaries separating these houses. Islam teaches that you are either a Muslim or you are on the other side. And what is the other side? It is the "House of War."

The final prophet. Muhammad is the last and final prophet. Moses was God's prophet for the Jews, and Jesus was God's prophet for the Christians. But Muhammad is God's prophet for all humanity. The Qur'an is the last word dictated by God, and a literal interpretation of the Qur'an is to be accepted. There is no place for critical thinking or evaluation. For how can a human being question Allah?

Opposition to Israel. Egyptian Sheikh Muhammad Al-Gamei'a was the United States' representative of Egypt's Al-Azhar University, and he also served as Imam of the Islamic Cultural Center and Mosque of New York City. Shortly after the World Trade Center attack, he left the United States and returned to Egypt. Sadly, this cleric, who is typical of many educated Muslims in the Middle East, began repeating the false claim circulating in Muslim circles that Israel was really behind the attack. He announced, "The Jewish element is as Allah described it when he said, 'They disseminate corruption in the land.' We know that they have always broken agreements, unjustly murdered the prophets, and betrayed the faith. Can they be expected to live up to their contracts with us? These people murdered the prophets; do you think they will stop spilling our blood? No."

The basis for such animosity toward Israel and the Jewish people comes from statements in the Qur'an, the Hadith, and Muslim tradition. The Qur'an says, "Fight those who do not believe" (Sura 9:29). It also says, "When you meet unbelievers, it is [a matter of] smiting necks. Then after you have cowed them with much slaughter, fasten the bonds tight!" (Sura 47:4). Perhaps most telling is the picture of warfare that, it is said, must come between Jews and Muslims in the final days. "The last hour would not come till the Muslims fight against the Jews and the Muslims kill them, until the Jews hide themselves, and the stones and trees would speak up saying, 'There is a Jew hiding behind me, come and kill him'" (Saying of the Prophet, Hadith Sahih Muslim, Book 40 #6985). Those Muslims who follow the Qur'an will never accept the State of Israel on soil once conquered for Allah. They can never rest until Israel has been abolished.

Yossi Klein Halevi reported in the *Jerusalem Post* on an interview with a Muslim named Karam who argued that America and Israel were trying to resist an inevitable historical process. "Everyone knows that in the end the whole world is going to become Muslims," reported Karam. Halevi asked, "And what will happen to the State of Israel?" Another young man who was listening to the conversation interrupted with his answer. "Israel? Israel will be the world capital of Islam."

Jihad. The Qur'an teaches that Muslims are to engage in *jihad*. The word *jihad* means "exertion" or "striving." It refers first to one's struggle in his or her own soul as he or she tries to submit to God. But the word also refers to the struggle Muslims will face with the world as they seek to spread the teaching of Islam.

Jihad can be used both in a spiritual sense and in a physical sense. In a physical sense, *jihad* is permitted when Muslims themselves are attacked, when their family or friends are attacked, when their nation is attacked, when their religion is attacked, or when oppression must be overcome. Modern Muslim scholar Ali Issa Othman states that physical struggle has always been a part of the spread of Islam. "The spread of Islam was military. There is a tendency to apologize for this, and we should not. It is one of the injunctions of the Qur'an that you must fight for the spreading of Islam." Similarly, Professor Fazulur Rahman suggests that, given the Muslim goal of building a just society on earth, "Jihad becomes an absolute necessity. How can such an ideological world-order be brought into existence without such means?"

Christians must distinguish between what Islam teaches and what is actually practiced by the majority of Muslims. We all know that there are Jewish people who do not observe the teachings of the Law, who are not "observant Jews." In the same way, there are individuals who call themselves Christians but who do not follow the Bible or have a personal relationship with Jesus Christ. So also there are Muslims who do not believe or practice all the teachings of Islam. They are Muslims by birth or family relationship but not by practice.

Most Muslims were appalled at the terrorist attack on the World Trade Center and the Pentagon. Those acts are as foreign to their beliefs as they are to ours. The vast majority of Muslims would never support terrorism. They are not Islamic fundamentalists. But the number who are is increasing. And there are countries where those who hold to these beliefs now control the whole population.

But the issue is not what the majority of Muslims believe. Rather, the issue is what the Qur'an teaches. Islamic fundamentalism is a relatively small branch of Islam, but it is growing because it resonates so closely with the teachings of the Qur'an.

Why have so few Islamic scholars risen up to denounce the human rights abuses and terrorist activities being committed in the name of Allah? Why have Muslim clerics throughout the Islamic world not been open and blunt in their condemnation of terrorist acts like the attacks on the World Trade Center and Pentagon, or the murder of innocent civilians in Jerusalem? Most of these religious leaders have not arisen to condemn such acts because the acts were done in the name of *jihad,* and such actions are commanded in the Qur'an and in the Hadith.

America is a mobile society. One morning you can awaken in Dallas; and four hours later you can be standing in New York City. Later that same day you can fly to Los Angeles and arrive in time for dinner. The United States is a nation of individuals who treasure personal freedom . . . and who believe in an inalienable right to "life, liberty, and the pursuit of happiness." It is hard for Americans to imagine that there are up to one billion people in the world who do not share the same mind-set. Americans are a free people who want to think freely. But true Muslims are expected to submit to the teachings of the Qur'an.

THE BATTLE OF GOG AND MAGOG

Islamic fundamentalism is the glue binding together the many groups who are part of the Al Qaeda terrorist organization. This strict form of Islam has also motivated terrorist attacks against the United States and against Israel. But with the worldwide coalition against terrorism gaining momentum, will the influence of Islamic fundamentalism decline? Is there a future for Islamic fundamentalism, or is it destined to die off in an increasingly secular world?

One key Scripture passage that can help us understand the future of Islamic fundamentalism is Ezekiel 38–39. This passage describes a unique attack against Israel by a coalition of nations. In the passage, God told Ezekiel to prophesy against "Gog, of the land of Magog, the chief prince of Meshech and Tubal" (38:2). Ezekiel announced that God would "turn you around, put hooks in your jaws and bring you out with your whole army" to attack the land of Israel (v. 4). This coalition of nations would also include several other allies. "Persia, Cush and Put will be with them, all with shields and helmets, also Gomer with all its troops, and Beth Togarmah from the far north with all its troops—the many nations with you" (vv. 5–6).

From the day Ezekiel announced this attack until today, no such invasion has ever taken place. But that should not surprise us because God specifically stated that the battle belonged to a very special time in history: "After many days you will be called to arms. In future years you will invade a land that has recovered from war, whose people were gathered from many nations to the mountains of Israel, which had long been desolate. They had been brought out from the nations, and now all of them live in safety" (v. 8). This attack will occur when the Jewish people have been regathered from the nations and are living securely in the land of Israel.

To understand the prophecy of Ezekiel 38–39, one must first understand where the countries named by Ezekiel are located on a map. "Magog," "Meshech," and "Tubal" were located around the Black and Caspian Seas in areas that were recently controlled by the former Soviet Union. More than 70 million people live in that area today. "Gomer" and "Togarmah" were located in what is today eastern Turkey.

Amazingly, these areas still share common religious and economic ties. In fact, Turkey continues to build economic relationships with the Muslim states that were once part of the Soviet Union.

Ezekiel listed three additional nations in verse 5—"Persia, Cush and Put." Ancient Persia is modern-day Iran, which continues to play a major role in exporting Islamic fundamentalism to the Muslim states in the former Soviet Union. Ancient Persia extended into the area now ruled by Pakistan. In Ezekiel's day, Cush was the nation to the south of Egypt. Today it is the country of Sudan, another state known for its Islamic fundamentalism. Put was the land to the west of Egypt, which today is Libya.

Over the past five years, I have returned to Pakistan several times. I'm amazed at the many business alliances between the states I have just named that are not reported in the Western media because—at least prior to September 11—the alliances had no immediate impact on the West. Since the events were taking place "over there," they were not seen to be that important. Terrorism also seemed far away. Americans were huddling and cuddling in the safety of this great nation. But over the course of a few hours, our perception of their importance changed. The economic alliances, the power struggles, the partnerships, the open communication, and the rise of terrorist groups based on Islamic fundamentalism have been developing for the last decade. We just didn't realize it.

A Future Role for Islam

Pakistan, Iran, and Turkey are historic allies. They have signed treaties that have focused on economic and military cooperation. And they will not back away from agreements that are in their mutual best interests. Ezekiel 38–39 teaches that a coalition of countries from specific areas—land that today includes Turkey, the former Soviet Muslim Republics,

Iran, Sudan, and Libya—will play a major role in an end-time attack against Israel. Though the Bible does not say what will bind these nations together, one possibility today could be the growing presence of Islamic fundamentalism with its hatred of Israel and its acceptance of *jihad*. The goal of Islamic fundamentalism is to re-create another Islamic kingdom whose laws are based on the Qur'an, to reconquer land that once belonged to Allah, and to attack the forces that oppose Islam . . . especially those of Christianity and Judaism.

Though Iran, Afghanistan, and a few other countries have tried to start an Islamic revolution, they have not yet been able to usher in a new Golden Age of Islam. Muslims have never forgotten that Kamal Ataturk abolished the Caliphate (Islamic kingdom) that was the Ottoman Empire and established in its place the modern State of Turkey. This was a turning point in the modern history of Islam. Since the end of the Ottoman Empire, many in the Muslim world believe they have lost the respect and honor that they deserve as followers of Allah.

The last century saw major political and geographical shifts throughout the world. The Soviet Union rose to power as the godless "Evil Empire" only to suffer a sudden collapse brought about, in part, by its humiliating military defeat in Afghanistan. The Muslims along the southern edge of the Soviet Union reasserted their independence and their identification as Muslims within the Muslim community. Turkey threw off the Ottoman Empire and became a secular state, only to see a rising threat within the state from Islamic extremists.

The West tried to impose its secular form of law and government on many Muslim countries in the last century. At times, they also carved the land up into separate countries based on artificial geographical boundaries. But the West was caught off guard by the shifting geopolitical forces of Islam. The artificial boundaries—and the secular forms of government—could not stand against the tide of Islam. Talat Tajidin, the mufti of Russia, declared, "We, Soviet Muslims, affirm that we were and still are part of the Moslem [nation]. . . . The Moslem world is not a geographical conception but a huge international power."

Muhammad Iqbal was a religious philosopher in Pakistan in the early twentieth century who began to dream of a new Islamic world. He stated a maxim that "religion without power is only philosophy." The Islamic fundamentalism that has developed from his teaching has a supernatural element as part of its core. These Muslim fundamentalists believe they have a divine mandate to accomplish because they possess God's final revelation. Since Muhammad and Islam are for everyone, whatever came before must be abrogated. The Bible is a corrupt book that was changed by the Christians. Allah has decreed that Islam will replace Judaism and Christianity, and it will conquer the world. And Muslims' holy quest is to bring it to pass.

God's Deliverance

After painting such a dark picture, I need to remind you that there is hope. There is hope for the people of Israel, and there is hope for us. Having described the attack against Israel in Ezekiel 38:1–9, the prophet then announced that God will come to rescue His own people. He will use an "earthquake," the invaders' own "sword," "plague and bloodshed," and "torrents of rain, hailstones and burning sulfur" (38:19–22) to destroy this invading army. God—and God alone—will put an end to this invasion. Regardless of the size of the army coming to attack Israel, God promises to intervene and defend His people . . . and to defeat the enemy. One result of the battle is that Israel will come to faith in her God. "From that day forward the house of Israel will know that I am the LORD their God" (39:22).

Before you become too discouraged, remember that God is in control. If you watch events in the Middle East or study the goals of Islamic fundamentalism, it would be easy for you to conclude that everything in the world is falling apart. But that is not true. God still rules from heaven . . . and His plan for the world is still being accomplished.

God will permit the nations named in Ezekiel 38 to unite together to accomplish their evil purpose. It is very possible that these nations will attack under the banner of Islam. But God also promised that He will destroy those nations just when victory seems to be within their grasp. His purpose for doing this is to reveal to the world that the God of the Bible, not the god of Islam, is the one true God. "I will make known my holy name among my people Israel. I will no longer let my holy name be profaned, and the nations will know that I the LORD am the Holy One in Israel" (39:7).

In John 14:6 Jesus said, "I am the way and the truth and the life. No one comes to the Father except through me." If Jesus is right, then He is the only way for humanity to come to God. Salvation does not come through Muhammad, Buddha, Krishna, or any other religious system. Those leaders are gone, but we worship a living Savior, One who has promised to come again to take His followers to heaven, and then to return to this earth to rule as "KING OF KINGS AND LORD OF LORDS" (Revelation 19:16).

These are the promises of the Lord Jesus Christ. That is the hope we have as believers. We do not need to live in fear. We know what the future holds because the God of all eternity has revealed it to us.

How Should We Respond?

So what should our response be to Muslims today? Should we view them as enemies? Should we respond to the events of September 11 by lashing back in anger at those who share the religion of the terrorists? No! For to do so is to deny the love and power of God expressed so clearly in John 3:16, "For God so loved the world that he gave his one and only Son, that whoever believes in him [including Muslims!] shall not perish but have eternal life." Muslims need to hear the gospel—the good news about Jesus Christ. They need to know the Savior. They need to understand God's love and care for them by seeing it demonstrated through us.

September 11 has opened many doors into the Muslim community. Large numbers of Muslims reacted with horror to those awful deeds committed in the name of their religion. And it has caused some to question the "truths" on which Islam is founded. This is the ideal time for Christians to reach out and display the unique message of love, forgiveness, and freedom that can only be found in Jesus Christ.

Let me conclude with a brief testimony to God's power. Just as the United States began sending troops to Pakistan, a riot broke out; and sixteen Christians were killed in Pakistan while worshiping in a church. Days later, I received a message that nineteen Afghans in Pakistan had accepted Jesus Christ as their Lord and Savior and were now ready to be baptized. The message continued, "We have to find secure water in a secure place to baptize them." This is not sensationalism. Though Satan might be at work, do not assume that everything is hopeless. God is working, too . . . and the power of Satan is no match for the power of God.

There is no power on heaven or on earth that can shake us. As Paul so confidently proclaimed, "For I am convinced that neither death nor life, neither angels nor demons, neither the present nor the future, nor any powers, neither height nor depth, nor anything else in all creation, will be able to separate us from the love of God that is in Christ Jesus our Lord" (Romans 8:38–39). No power in existence can deter us from our mission, and our mission from God is to proclaim salvation through Jesus Christ, and Him alone.

We must never give up. Though many may have to sacrifice their lives for the sake of the gospel, we will continue on because the victory has already been won on the Cross. We love, worship, and serve an awesome God who brings hope, not misery . . . who brings salvation, not bondage. Someday "at the name of Jesus every knee should bow, in heaven and on earth and under the earth, and every tongue confess that Jesus Christ is Lord, to the glory of God the Father" (Philippians 2:10–11).

I have not come across any passage of Scripture that says the Great Commission excludes Muslims. They need Jesus Christ. The end times will come according to God's own schedule. The battle described in Ezekiel 38–39 will take place. And it is very possible that the nations involved will be united because of their common belief in Islamic fundamentalism. In the meantime, we have a mission to accomplish. That mission is to preach Jesus Christ, God's Son, crucified, raised from the dead, victorious, and coming again. Salvation is only found in His name.

Pastor Ian Freestone, who serves in the Ruach Neighbourhood Churches in Sydney, Australia, best described the reaction believers ought to have to Muslims; and I will end with his passionate call to arms . . . arms folded in prayer, reaching out in love, and active in service for Christ.

> If we as Christians had half the outrage of Islamic extremists and expressed it, not in violence but in earnest prayer to God and practical support for our suffering brothers and sisters, then perhaps the world would see our love for one another. So I suggest that whilst we should on one hand be concerned at the rise of Islamic extremism, the answer is to get a bit extreme ourselves. I'm talking about being an extreme follower of Jesus Christ, consumed with love for our brothers

and sisters, consumed with love for those who do not know the Lord and consumed with love for those who would persecute the name of Christ. Forget "terrorist cells." How about cells of Christian communities, terrorizing the Kingdom of darkness with the love of God?[1]

NOTE

1. Christian Aid's *Missions Insider Report,* Nov. 6. 2001, vol. 2, no. 44.

4 WHEN ALL HELL BREAKS LOOSE

Dr. Erwin W. Lutzer

When Lucifer, (whose name means "light bearer"), rolled the dice, gambling that he could do better by being God's enemy than God's friend, he set in motion a moral catastrophe that would reverberate throughout the universe. You and I have been deeply affected by his decision made in the ages long ago.

What may not be widely known is that Lucifer was already defeated the moment he sinned. He was defeated strategically, since as one of God's creatures he would be forced to depend upon God for his continued existence. Any power he would exercise would always be subject to God's will and decree. Thus, moment by moment, he would suffer the humiliation of knowing that he could never be the ultimate cause of his existence and power.

To clarify, I don't simply mean to say that for every move he would make God would make a countermove. That was true, of course; but the situation for Satan would be more ominous, because he cannot even now make his own first move without God's express will and consent!

Let us boldly affirm that whatever mischief Satan is allowed to do, it is always appointed by God for the ultimate service and benefit to the saints. William Gurnall, after encouraging believers to hold fast to the assurance that God is watching Satan's every move, and will not let him have the final victory, writes, "When God says 'Stay!' he must stand like a dog by the table while the saints feast on God's comfort. He does not dare to snatch even a tidbit, for the Master's eye is always upon him."[1] And so it is; our Master's eye is ever upon him. After his first act of disobedience, his failure and doom were sealed.

According to Isaiah's account, Lucifer wanted to be "like the Most High" (Isaiah 14:14). In what sense did he think he could achieve this goal? He certainly could never be omnipresent or omniscient. He knew that he could be "like God" only in one respect: He wanted independence. What he did not know was that he would still have to exist under the authority of God's will and decree. How much power does the devil have? Just as much as God allows him to have and not one whit more!

Even as you read these words, Satan is a hapless player in the drama that he himself set in motion. And there is nothing he can do to change the outcome.

I'm convinced that unless we grasp how the devil fits into God's scheme of things, we will find it more difficult to stand against his conspiracy against us personally and his influence within our culture. How we perceive our enemy will largely determine how we fight against him. We must live with the unshakable confidence not only that God will win in the end, but that He is actually winning even now, day by day.

As we shall see, the biblical portrait of Satan is that he does indeed have great power, but it is always limited by the purposes and plans of God. It is a picture of a proud being who has already been humbled. It is the picture of a being whose greatest asset in his war with us is our own ignorance.

THE FINAL PHASES OF SATAN'S CAREER

Let's look at the final three phases of Satan's career. Three times in the book of Revelation he is "thrown down" as the curtain closes. Each round is more humiliating and torturous than the preceding one. First, he is *thrown* from heaven to earth (12:9); then he is *thrown* from earth into the Abyss (20:3); and finally he is *thrown* into the lake of fire (20:10). The proud being who thought it would be to his advantage to stand against God will have to endure an eternity of humiliation.

During the coming Tribulation period, there will be a flurry of demonic activity. For example, under the fifth trumpet, hordes of demonic spirits from the Abyss will occasion such agonizing torture that "men will seek death, but will not find it; they will long to die, but death will elude them" (Revelation 9:6). Under the sixth trumpet, an army of 200 million strong will decimate a third of the world's population in terrifying judgments (vv. 13–16).

But worse is to come.

Let's describe three snapshots of Satan's last stand. Yes, as we shall see, by the time all hell breaks loose, the end is near.

The Devil Is Thrown Out of Heaven

In Revelation 12 we are invited behind the scenes to witness two signs that introduce us to a great eschatological drama. "A great and wondrous sign appeared in heaven: a woman clothed with the sun, with the moon under her feet and a crown of twelve stars on her head" (v. 1). This woman is in travail, about to give birth to a child.

This woman represents Israel, the twelve stars being a symbol of the twelve tribes. The sun and moon remind us of Joseph's dream in which these heavenly bodies represented his parents, Jacob and Rachel (Genesis 37:9–10). Further evidence that this is Israel is the fact that this woman will still be in existence during the great Tribulation period. She is about to give birth to a son "who will rule all the nations with an iron scepter. And her child was snatched up to God and to his throne" (Revelation 12:5). This is a one-sentence summary of Christ's birth, life, and ascension into heaven.

A second "sign" appears in this drama: that of a great red dragon "with seven heads and ten horns and seven crowns on his heads" (v. 3). The crowns represent Satan's authority; the ten horns evidently are the ten kingdoms described in Daniel 7:7–8 that refer to a unified Europe ruled under Satan's puppet, the Antichrist. The dragon who controls this political/religious system is red, perhaps a reminder that Satan is a murderer.

And there is more. "His tail swept a third of the stars out of the sky and flung them to the earth" (v. 4). If these stars are angelic beings, as seems likely, then this passage is a flashback to Satan's fall when innumerable angels followed him in his rebellion against God. John sees past, present, and future events all brought together in a kaleidoscope.

The picture is intended to be grotesque. This evil dragon stands by waiting for the woman to give birth so that he can devour the child. We think immediately of Herod who tried to slay Christ when He was born in Bethlehem. This was the first in a series of attempts Satan made to kill the Christ.

The child escapes, of course. Mary, Joseph, and the child flee into Egypt to thwart Herod's plans; and when they return to Nazareth, Jesus is raised in their home like a normal child. Later He reveals Himself to be the Messiah, is rejected, and is crucified for the sins of the world. Then He is raised from the dead and taken up into heaven, just as this passage teaches.

> And there was war in heaven. Michael and his angels fought against the dragon, and the dragon and his angels fought back. But he was not strong enough, and they lost their place in heaven. The great dragon was hurled down— that ancient serpent called the devil, or Satan, who leads the whole world astray. He was hurled to the earth, and his angels with him. (Revelation 12:7–9)

Does Satan have access to heaven today? Some teach that Satan was cast out of heaven when Christ died on the cross. However, in context, it is more likely that Satan, although defeated at the Cross, is thrown out of heaven in the middle of the Tribulation period.

If Satan does have access to heaven today, as I believe he does, it is to continue his ongoing dialogue with God about us. Specifically, he comes to accuse, to cajole, and to receive permission to harass people on earth as God gives him permission. Though he is at war with all of humanity, his special attacks are aimed at those whom he knows will belong to God forever. Conceivably, dialogues such as those in the book of Job are happening today.

And now the best part.

Though Michael had so much respect for Satan that he would not contend with him over the body of Moses (Jude 9), he now fights with unerring confidence. "Michael and his angels fought against the dragon. . . . But he [the dragon] was not strong enough, and they lost their place in heaven" (Revelation 12:7–8). Let's not forget that at one time Michael and Lucifer were colleagues; they served the same Master and had essentially the same responsibilities. Since it is likely that Michael at one time served under

Lucifer, the loss of this battle was especially painful for the devil. He was thrown out of heaven by one who at one time had been his underling! How humiliating!

This is the heavenly counterpart to Christ's victory on earth. The victory of the Cross is now translated into a victory in heaven. The open display of Satan's defeat is now translated into reality. The devil and his angels are thrown out and "[lose] their place in heaven." The Serpent glances toward heaven for the last time and knows that for him the gates are now bolted shut. He does not leave heaven willingly but is *thrown* to the earth by someone stronger than he.

Imagine his anger when he sees the gates of heaven close, with the saints he had persecuted on earth now standing before the throne of God in the spotless beauty of Jesus! He sees them exalted above the angels, as brothers of Christ, though they had committed many of the same sins as he. He knows that they will be there forever; he also knows where he will be forever. No wonder he is furious.

All hell now breaks loose.

First, he attacks Israel. He who has always desired to destroy the Promised Seed so that the purposes and plans of God might not be fulfilled, makes one last attempt to exterminate the nation of Israel. Pursuing the woman, the Serpent originates a flood to sweep the woman away, but the earth swallows up the water (Revelation 12:15–16). Whatever this might mean, it is clear that it is one last satanic effort to destroy the nation. In some way, God assists the Israelites so that they are not completely wiped out.

Then, having failed at his extermination of Israel, Satan turns his attention to the believers who are in existence, "Then the dragon was enraged at the woman and went off to make war against the rest of her offspring—those who obey God's commandments and hold to the testimony of Jesus" (v. 17).

Finally, Satan focuses on his political agenda and reaches out to rule the world. Losing his place in heaven made him only more determined to succeed on earth. During the last three-and-one-half years of the Tribulation period, Satan, through the Antichrist, rules the world. Though he knows his time is short, he wants to make the most of it. We read these stunning words: "He was given power to make war against the saints and to conquer them. And he was given authority over every tribe, people, language and nation. All inhabitants of the earth will worship the beast—all whose names have not been written in the book of life belonging to the Lamb that was slain from the creation of the world" (Revelation 13:7–8).

By the time the Antichrist appears, the world will be ready to deify a leader if he appears to have what it takes to unite the world and bring in an era of peace. It is not enough for Satan to inhabit a man who will claim to be God. The master deceiver will actually try to duplicate the three members of the Trinity. These three personalities will do their best to try to confuse the world by pretending to be the true and living God.

First, Satan himself corresponds to God the Father, and he is spoken of as the "dragon" who gives his authority to the Beast who is the Antichrist (Revelation 13:4). Thus Satan wants to receive the worship that is due only the Almighty. This dream, now within reach, will shortly become a nightmare.

Second, there is the Beast who is empowered by the Dragon, who corresponds to Christ. He will try his best to do miracles and duplicate Christ's resurrection. Specifically we read, "One of the heads of the beast seemed to have had a fatal wound, but the fatal wound had been healed. The whole world was astonished and followed the beast" (v. 3). The world will believe that the Antichrist survived a wound that would have put any other man to death. The skeptical will be convinced that this is the man to follow and worship.

At last there will be religious unity. The Dragon and the Beast will receive the worship of the world. Yes, all who dwell upon the earth will worship him, except the elect whose names were written in the Book of Life from before the foundation of the world (v. 8). Apart from the relatively few who will have the courage to oppose this dictator, he will capture the hearts of the world.

During the apex of Hitler's career, the Lord's Prayer was changed by many to read, "Our Father Adolf who art in Nuremberg, the Third Reich come." In the same way, people will worship the Antichrist who has had the financial wizardry to put the world on a stable economic base. He will be the one who is deemed worthy of the praise accorded him.

The third member of this unholy trinity is referred to as "another beast" in Revelation 13:11. Just as the Holy Spirit draws attention to Christ, so the assignment of this evil man is to get the world to worship the Antichrist. He "made the earth and its inhabitants worship the first beast, whose fatal wound had been healed" (v. 12). To gain the confidence of the world, this beast performs great miracles. Many of these wonders performed by this unholy triad are specified: Fire will come down from heaven (v. 13); images will be caused to speak (v. 15, though possibly this will be accomplished through trickery since it is unlikely that Satan can create life); and the fatal wound will be healed (v. 3).

By duplicating the miracles of Christ, the world will believe. Satan's fondest wish will be realized. The whole world is worshiping his man; and behind the man is Satan, who has longed for absolute control.

Now that Satan's puppet is in place, he will be able to rule the world through a vast financial network based on stringent controls. No one will be able to buy or sell without the "mark of the beast." Those who challenge his authority will be put to death. Also like Hitler, the new messiah will hate the Jews with a vengeance.

This, then, is the culmination to which all the various strands of religious unity are headed. Even the tributaries of satanic worship that we see today might be the very ones that will flow into a single river of occult religion. Here is the apex of the godhood of man. At last, the problems of the world will be overcome, with spiritual solutions.

Under the guise of laudable slogans, the deification of man will reach its most striking affirmation. All opposition will be set aside, and the New World Order will be in place.

For those who do not get on board, there will be intimidation, starvation, and liquidation.

- When all hell breaks loose, there will be worldwide deception.
- When all hell breaks loose, there will be worldwide control.
- When all hell breaks loose, there will be worldwide blasphemy.

A furious devil is in charge—but not for long.

The Devil Is Thrown into the Abyss

This time the conflict between Christ and the devil will not take place in the Judean hills, but on the Mount of Olives. Satan will not confront a Christ who is weakened by hunger, but a glorified Christ who comes suited for war. The rightful Ruler is on His way, and Satan knows it.

Zechariah wrote,

> I will gather all the nations to Jerusalem to fight against it; the city will be captured, the houses ransacked, and the women raped. Half of the city will go into exile, but the rest

of the people will not be taken from the city. Then the LORD will go out and fight against those nations, as he fights in the day of battle. On that day his feet will stand on the Mount of Olives, east of Jerusalem, and the Mount of Olives will split in two from east to west, forming a great valley, with half of the mountain moving north and half moving south. (14:2–4)

Catch your breath as you read a parallel passage in Revelation 19. There we learn that we will follow Christ to subdue the nations of the earth in the final battle of history! "The armies of heaven were following him, riding on white horses and dressed in fine linen, white and clean" (v. 14). We will ride with Him to victory and stand with Him on the Mount of Olives. Those believers who have never had the good fortune to visit the land of Israel in this life will get the grand tour in the next. Christ Himself shall lead His people into victory.

As for the Beast and the False Prophet, they are now "thrown alive into the fiery lake of burning sulfur" (Revelation 19:20). Satan will share their fate but not just yet. He still has one intermediate stop before he joins those whom he so cruelly deceived and controlled. The kingdom age is about to dawn, and God still needs him to fulfill a final purpose. The fact that he is spared the lake of fire for now does not make his future there any less certain. History now marches with inevitable certainty.

When Christ confronted the demon-possessed man who lived among the tombs, the demons begged that they might not be cast into the Abyss because they feared being tormented before their time (Luke 8:31). Christ granted their request and allowed them to enter a herd of swine, which then promptly ran into the Sea of Galilee and were drowned.

But the demons were able only to postpone, not cancel, their impending doom. Now that the kingdom is established under its rightful King, Satan and those who are his are for a time confined to the Abyss which they so much feared.

> And I saw an angel coming down out of heaven, having the key to the Abyss and holding in his hand a great chain. He seized the dragon, that ancient serpent, who is the devil, or Satan, and bound him for a thousand years. He threw him into the Abyss, and locked and sealed it over him, to keep him from deceiving the nations anymore until the thousand years were ended. After that, he must be set free for a short time. (Revelation 20:1–3)

Why are Satan and his demons bound? One more time God will demonstrate the bankruptcy of the human heart. Though Satan is not allowed to deceive the nations during Christ's reign, the nations are still led astray by the inherent wickedness of human nature. So after Satan is loosed at the end of the thousand years, he finds those who are willing to side with him in one final assault on God (vv. 7–9).

Jay Adams, whose books on counseling have been helpful to many, believes that even now we are in the kingdom age and that Satan is bound. This curtailment or restraint, he says, "involved the virtual cessation of such activity [demonic possession] by his demonic forces. This accounts for the rare incidence, if not the entire absence of demonic possession in modern times."[2]

I disagree.

If the first step in Satan's demise is that he is forbidden to reside in heaven, then the second step is that he is forbidden to reside on earth. For a thousand years, the nations are permitted to go their own way without satanic direction or influence.

Satan's remorse is now magnified. Milton captured this despairing sense of permanent isolation from God. "Which way I fly is Hell; myself am Hell." He who had always taken his own hell with him, now is about to be cast into a hell of a different sort. Satan must now relinquish control of all beings he ever had influenced. The power is gone; so is the insolence, the scheming, and the defiance. Stripped of everything he once thought he had, he is now forced to abide in eternal shame.

The Devil Is Thrown into the Lake of Fire

We are now ready for the final stage in Satan's demise. "And the devil, who deceived them, was thrown into the lake of burning sulfur, where the beast and the false prophet had been thrown. They will be tormented day and night for ever and ever" (Revelation 20:10). At last, Satan joins his cohorts in eternal torment. No doubt he will discover that it is even worse than he imagined.

What can we say about the eternal state of Satan in the lake of fire? First, this place was created by God, prepared by the Almighty for the inhabitants who were doomed to indwell it. Christ said that God will say to the wicked, "Depart from me, you who are cursed, into the eternal fire prepared for the devil and his angels" (Matthew 25:41).

God has prepared two eternal destinies. "I am going . . . to prepare a place for you," Christ told His disciples (John 14:2). That place, heaven, is even now ready to receive those who will be with God forever. As for the lake of fire, it has also been prepared. Though no one is yet in hell today (the unbelieving dead go to hades), Christ implies that the lake of fire has nevertheless already been prepared. Though now empty, it is being readied in anticipation of its occupants.

Let us say boldly that the lake of fire is not simply a spin-off of the natural creation, but is actually a specific place created for a specific reason. And the Creator rules whatever He creates. Not even here does God abandon His sovereign rule. If the devil is God's devil, then hell is God's hell.

God, not the devil, rules in hell. He is the Creator, and He does not give a part of His kingdom to another. Hell is neither the figment of a lively imagination, nor is it the place where Satan will have his kingdom. God is in the heavens above; and because He is omnipresent, He is in hell below. Even there, properly interpreted, His will is done. Consider the following five facts about hell that require God to be in control.

First, hell is a place of judgment for the rebellion of God's creatures. The judgments of hell will be meticulously meted out, all under the watchful supervision of God. The penalties must be just, accurate, and commensurate with the offense. God would never delegate the delicate task of justice to another.

Second, hell is a place of torment. The impression, often given in medieval folklore, is that hell is the devil's domain. We get the idea that he rules there, giving orders to his own demons and harassing people at will. Dante painted a picture of hell with the demons tormenting those who arrive at this destination. Their pitchforks were thought to be a kind of medieval billy club used to inflict torture. This, of course, is based on mythology and not the Bible.

We must look at the text carefully. We read that "they will be tormented day and night for ever and ever" (Revelation 20:10). This is not where Satan torments others but where he is "tormented." He is not the tormentor but the *tormented.* He is scarcely in a position to trouble others, for he himself is overcome by the troubles heaped upon him.

The Serpent's state in hell is even more pitiful than that of other creatures! Those who have sinned greatly are punished greatly. No one sinned with more knowledge and more light than Lucifer. His judgment will be in line with his rebellion. Be assured there is no king in hell!

J. Marcellus Kik suggests, perhaps quite rightly,

> What a welcome will the Devil receive from those whom he has deceived! What curses, what vituperations, what abuses, what reviling, what berating will be heaped upon his head! He will be surrounded by a lake of curses. His nostrils cannot escape the stench of vituperation. It is part of his torment day and night. He will be hated, despised and rejected for all of eternity.[3]

Satan will never sing again; he will only howl. The memory of heaven's choirs will only magnify the torment of his own regret. And there is no exit.

Third, hell has many occupants. As we have already learned, the devil is thrown where "the beast and the false prophet had been thrown" (v. 10). They have been there since the return of Christ which, at this time, will have happened a thousand years before. So far as we know, they are hell's first occupants. No doubt the other fallen angels enter along with their master, Apollyon.

But hell also has human occupants. Those who are not sheltered from the wrath of God by Christ must bear their own fate. Immediately after the devil's arrival into the lake of fire, we read of the judgment of all unbelieving dead. They are judged according to their works. "If anyone's name was not found written in the book of life, he was thrown into the lake of fire" (v. 15).

Fourth, hell is eternal. Though many insist that hell is a place of annihilation, this simply does not do justice to the texts of Scripture. We are told that they are "tormented day and night for ever and ever." Unceasing restlessness; unceasing hopelessness; unceasing regret.

Christ taught that hell was as eternal as heaven. "Then they will go away to eternal punishment, but the righteous to eternal life" (Matthew 25:46). If we believe that we will enjoy eternal life forever, we must believe that others will suffer eternal punishment forever. Unfortunately, we are not free to choose our beliefs based on our preferences.

Fifth, hell is just. To us as humans, everlasting punishment is disproportionate to the offense committed. God appears to be cruel, unjust, sadistic, and vindictive. The purpose of punishment, we are told, is always redemptive. Rehabilitation is the goal of all prison sentences. The concept of a place where there will be everlasting punishment without any possibility of parole or reform seems unjust.

But we must remember that all beings, whether demonic or angelic, will be judged on the basis of knowledge. More will be required from those who have been given much. The Serpent, needless to say, cannot plead ignorance. His decision was made with a knowledge of the facts before him. Of course, he didn't know everything, since such full knowledge belongs only to God, but he knew enough to be severely judged for his stupidity.

God judges with full knowledge of all the facts. No motive will be misinterpreted; no extenuating circumstances will be overlooked. Unlike a human court that can shelve details or misinterpret them, God's knowledge extends both to that which has happened in the world as well as that which might have happened under different circumstances.

Satan and those who will join him in the lake of fire are eternally guilty. No suffering of the creature can ever repay the Creator. If suffering could erase even the most insignificant sin, then those in hell would eventually be freed after their debt was paid. But all creaturely suffering could not so much as cancel a single sin.

The cosmic gamble failed. He who would not be God's willing servant is now God's unwilling prisoner. He who wished to strut about the world is now confined to the parameters of hell. He who wished to rule others now finds that he cannot rule himself.

The destruction of the Serpent in the lake of fire stands as a final witness to the fact that no creature who fights against the Creator will win. No will pitted against the will of God will ever find permanent fulfillment and freedom. God has proven that He alone rules and beside Him there is no other.

A WORD TO THE OVERCOMERS

The devil's "last hurrah" has lessons for us in doing "spiritual warfare." For one thing, we must remember that "all hell cannot break loose" until heaven wills it. The devil rules today, but only by divine decree. He tempts us only to the extent that God chooses to grant him his wish. He destroys, but only as God approves of such destruction. He stalks proudly about, but only as far as God will let him. He is unwilling to face the reality of his impending eternal humiliation and shame. He already knows what others might not: His present battles are but a charade on the cosmic stage. The outcome is certain and unavoidable.

And how do we overcome the Evil One? Just as the saints will do in the Tribulation period, "They overcame him by the blood of the Lamb and by the word of their testimony; they did not love their lives so much as to shrink from death" (Revelation 12:11).

First, they will overcome him by the blood of the Lamb. Satan can no longer accuse those who have been acquitted by God, thanks to the sacrifice of Christ. Every unjust accusation is now silenced. As we read, "To him who loves us and has freed us from our sins by his blood" (Revelation 1:5). No matter how extensive Satan's end-time network, the power of the Cross still stands. Indeed, the power of the Cross is seen most clearly when the forces of evil seem to triumph.

Even those of us who have been schooled in the Christian

faith often do not grasp the significance of the blood of Christ, the basis for our forgiveness and victory. At the end of a difficult day of failure and sin, we are tempted to come to God, telling Him that we really don't expect to have our prayers answered because we have failed so miserably. In contrast, when we have had a good day, and our relationship with God appears to be on target, we think that surely God will hear us.

In both instances we err. Whether our day has been good or bad, our basis for approaching God is always the same, namely, the blood of Christ. And whether our guilt is objective, that is, the guilt that appears before God, or subjective, that is, the feelings of guilt we have within our own consciences, the remedy is always the same: the blood of Christ.

When Moses was in Egypt, the homes of the Israelites were spared because of the blood on their doors. It mattered not whether the families inside had a good day or a bad day; it mattered not whether they had been successful in overcoming sin, important though that was. What mattered was the blood. For God said, "When I see the blood, I will pass over you" (Exodus 12:13).

Second, these saints will overcome him by the "word of their testimony." The proclamation of the gospel—the assertion that Christ died for us and we have experienced His victory—this is what enables us to stand against the rage of Satan. This, after all, is the only hope for our country and our culture.

Third, they will overcome him by being willing to die for their faith. The gift of martyrdom is what also keeps Satan from winning a victory. John wrote, "They did not love their lives so much as to shrink from death" (Revelation 12:11). These believers die under the rule of a revived Roman Empire, just as the early Christians died under the rule of the original Roman Empire. In both cases, their martyrdom is what God has willed. Satanic forces might instigate the destroying; but God does the delegating. Just as it was God's will for Christ to die at the hands of evil men, so His followers die under the same care and providential plan. Even here, the devil is still God's servant.

As Luther wrote,

> *Let goods and kindred go,*
> *This mortal life also—*
> *The body they may kill;*
> *God's truth abideth still:*
> *His kingdom is forever.*

Death cannot frighten those who follow the Prince of Life.

"Oh, the depth of the riches of the wisdom and knowledge of God! How unsearchable his judgments, and his paths beyond tracing out! 'Who has known the mind of the Lord? Or who has been his counselor?' 'Who has ever given to God that God should repay him?' For from him and through him and to him are all things. To him be the glory forever! Amen" (Romans 11:33–36).

Soli Deo gloria!

(Portions of this chapter were adapted from *The Serpent of Paradise: The Incredible Story of How Satan's Rebellion Serves God's Purposes,* by Erwin W. Lutzer, Moody Press, 1996.)

NOTES

1. William Gurnall, ed. *The Christian in Complete Armour: Daily Readings in Spiritual Warfare* (Chicago: Moody, 1995).
2. Jay Adams, *The Big Umbrella* (Phillipsburg, N.J.: Presbyterian & Reformed, 1973), 118.
3. As quoted by Frederick S. Leahy in *Satan Cast Out* (Carlisle, Pa.: Banner of Truth Trust, 1975), 61.

5 FROM HERE TO ETERNITY

Dr. Mark L. Bailey

HISTORICAL PERSPECTIVE ON GOD'S REVELATION

On average, we all blink about twenty-five times every minute. Each blink takes one-fifth of a second. Therefore, if you take a ten-hour automobile trip, averaging only forty miles per hour, you drive twenty of those miles with your eyes closed. Just think how much you miss!

In the Time of the Patriarchs

Prophecy is a matter of perspective. Let's begin by thinking through the big picture of the prophetic Scriptures. In the patriarchal times, God revealed Himself and His will through what we might call theophanic revelation. A "theophany" is a vision or manifestation of God. One could argue that every theophany in the Old Testament was in reality a preincarnate appearance of Jesus Christ. He appeared outside the tent with Abraham (Genesis 18:1). Jacob wrestled with the Angel of the Lord (Genesis 32:22–30). Daniel reported that One who looked like "a son of the gods" appeared in the fiery furnace with the three Hebrew lads (Daniel 3:25).

In the Time of the Israelite Prophets

In prophetic times, we might call God's truth *theopneustic* revelation. We get "theopneustic" when we combine the word for God *(theos)* and the word for Spirit *(pneuma)*. Hence, through the prophets came the revelation of God's Spirit to God's people, and that message became known as the Word of the Lord.

In the Time of Christ

When we come to the New Testament, the Bible tells us that the Word became flesh and that which was eternal became personal (John 1:14). Jesus Christ is a *theanthropic* revelation of God. "Theanthropic" is the combination of the words for God *(theos)* and man *(anthropos)*. So theanthropic revelation came through the incarnation of the Son of God when He took on human flesh and revealed the Father by what He said and did.

In God's Revelation to the Church

In the books of the New Testament following the Gospels, we might have what we call *theologic* or theological revelation. This is the communication of God in truth—in written form. So, whether we're talking theophanic, theopneustic, theanthropic, or theological revelation, God's truth has been revealed to us in the panorama of the Scriptures. As a way of seeing God's perspective for the future, the purpose of this chapter is to suggest an overview in terms of a *day,* a *week,* and a *millennium.* From here to eternity, what does the future hold?

THE DAY OF THE LORD

Several years ago a movie appeared entitled *Twister*. The climax of the story focused on a group of Oklahoma storm chasers pursuing an F5 tornado with sustained winds of 261–316 miles per hour. A few years later the state of Oklahoma experienced a twister that could have inspired a sequel to the movie. On May 3, 1999, storm watchers located a large tornado in southwest Oklahoma. Unlike most tornadoes, this one did not break up, weaken, or disappear back into the clouds after a short time. "Over the next few hours, this 'routine' tornado metastasized into a monster without equal,"[1] one writer recorded.

The storm grew into an F5 tornado a half-mile wide that remained on the ground for an extended period of time as it cut a devastating sixty-mile swath of destruction through town after town, neighborhood after neighborhood. And when the steamrolling storm finally ran out of energy, it had totally destroyed fifteen hundred homes, damaged more than eight thousand others, and killed forty-four people. After the storm, the meteorologists determined that the wind speed generated by the tornado had peaked at 318 miles per hour. To this point in history those were the strongest winds ever recorded on the face of the globe. The storm was in a category all its own.

The Bible calls the future time of destruction and trouble that will target planet Earth "the Day of the Lord." Since September 11, 2001, all of us understand a little more clearly the impact that sudden destruction and loss of life can unleash on a nation. We have also seen the effect that this one tragedy has had around the world. Sociologists, psychologists, philosophers, and media pundits all agree: Life will never be quite the same on planet Earth. But there is a day coming on planet Earth that will cause tragedies like the Oklahoma City tornado or the events of September 11 to pale in comparison.

To help understand the scope of this coming disaster, let's assume that the world's population just prior to the start of the Day of the Lord will be exactly what it is today . . . about six billion people. The next event on God's prophetic calendar is the removal of the church from the earth. We do not know how many believers in Jesus Christ there are on the planet. But to be exceedingly generous, let's assume that as many as two billion inhabitants would have placed their faith in Jesus Christ. (The actual number, known only to God, is probably *much* smaller.) That would leave four billion people on the earth at the start of the Day of the Lord.

The book of Revelation records that God will unleash a series of judgments on the earth as Christ opens a seven-sealed document in heaven (Revelation 6). With the opening of the fourth seal, one-fourth of the world's population will be killed by "sword, famine and plague, and by the wild beasts of the earth" (v. 8). John later reports that an additional third of the earth's population will be killed (9:15). If four billion people are on Earth at the start of the Day of the Lord, at least two billion will die in a very short time as God exercises judgment on planet Earth. But what do we know about the Day of the Lord?

The Importance of the Day

The Day of the Lord is an important topic for two reasons. First, it is important because it is a frequent topic in God's prophetic Word. It occurs in thirteen of the sixteen writing prophets of the Old Testament. More than one hundred separate passages speak about "the day of the Lord," "a day for the Lord," or "that day." Second, it is important because of its ferocity. It will be the worst hour of human history. Jesus said in His discourse from the Mount of Olives that when this judgment takes place—especially in the latter half of the Tribulation period—it will be a time of "great distress, unequaled from the beginning of the world until now—and never to be equaled again" (Matthew 24:21).

The Bible says this coming day will be a worldwide period of testing on planet Earth—an "hour of trial that is going to come upon the whole world to test those who live on the earth" (Revelation 3:10). It will involve a world-terrorizing and world-intimidating series of judgments. The people on planet Earth will run to the hills to hide. It will make the Taliban retreat in Afghanistan look very insignificant. And the people hiding in the caves will be praying—not to God but to the rocks—asking them, "Fall on us and hide us from the face of him who sits on the throne and from the wrath of the Lamb! For the great day of their wrath has come, and who can stand?" (Revelation 6:16–17).

A Period of Time

The Day of the Lord is a period of time when God's judgment and salvation are revealed, a time when He directly intervenes in history. If one looks at the concept of a "day" from a Jewish perspective, it is composed of two parts: an evening and a morning. That is why, at the time of the earth's first created day, we read, "And there was evening, and there was morning—the first day" (Genesis 1:5). In essence, we can divide a day into two parts. There is darkness on the one half; there is light on the other. And the same is true for the period of time referred to as the Day of the Lord.

The darkness represents the judgment that will come during a seven-year period known as the Tribulation. The

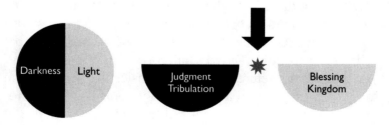

light represents a period of blessing that will be the kingdom age or, as it is called because of its length, the Millennium —the thousand-year reign of Christ on earth. Several passages of Scripture talk about the Day of the Lord as a period of judgment or blessing.

A time of judgment. The prophet Zephaniah described the Day of the Lord as a time of darkness and judgment.

> The great day of the LORD is near—near and coming quickly. Listen! The cry on the day of the LORD will be bitter, the shouting of the warrior there. That day will be a day of wrath, a day of distress and anguish, a day of trouble and ruin, a day of darkness and gloom, a day of clouds and blackness, a day of trumpet and battle cry against the fortified cities and against the corner towers. I will bring distress on the people and they will walk like blind men, because they have sinned against the LORD. (Zephaniah 1:14–17a)

One of the purposes for the Tribulation period, or the Day of the Lord, is to bring retribution against sin. Zephaniah continued, "Their blood will be poured out like dust and their entrails like filth. Neither their silver nor their gold will be able to save them on the day of the LORD's wrath. In the fire of his jealousy the whole world will be consumed, for he will make a sudden end of all who live in the earth" (1:17b–18).

A time of blessing. But the prophets also announced that there would be blessing in the Day of the Lord. For example, Amos predicted, "In that day I will restore David's fallen tent. I will repair its broken places, restore its ruins, and build it as it used to be" (Amos 9:11). If God promises that He is going to build David's fallen tent "as it used to be," then this is not a reference to God transferring the kingdom from an earthly one to a heavenly one. Nor is it a description of some form of spiritualized kingdom in existence in the present age of the church, as some teach. Rather, God is announcing that there is going to be an earthly, Davidic kingdom on planet Earth, "as it used to be."

But what is the purpose for the restoration of an earthly, Davidic kingdom? God seems to provide the answer when He says, "'so that they may possess the remnant of Edom and all the nations that bear my name,' declares the LORD, who will do these things. 'The days are coming,' declares the LORD, 'when the reaper will be overtaken by the plowman and the planter by the one treading grapes. New wine will drip from the mountains and flow from all the hills'" (Amos 9:12–13). The kingdom must come in that day so God can fulfill the promises He made to the patriarchs and to David. Even the land will experience God's promised blessings in that day. The laborers will be bumping into one another out in the fields because the crops will grow so rapidly that the laborers will not know whether they are planting or reaping. That will prove to be one great harvesttime!

Another great purpose for the restoration of an earthly, Davidic kingdom is to restore Israel to her homeland. "'I will bring back my exiled people Israel; they will rebuild the ruined cities and live in them. They will plant vineyards and drink their wine; they will make gardens and eat their fruit. I will plant Israel in their own land, never again to be uprooted from the land I have given them,' says the LORD your God" (vv. 14–15).

There is judgment in the Day of the Lord, and there is salvation in the Day of the Lord. The great event that separates the nighttime from the daytime is the "sunrise." When the Lord returns to earth after the Tribulation, the Bible speaks of Him as "the sun of righteousness [who] will rise with healing in its wings" (Malachi 4:2). While the Day of the Lord is a period of time, that specific point in time when the "sun of righteousness . . . will rise" is also referred to as the Day of the Lord.

A Point in Time

The Day of the Lord is a period of time that includes judgment and blessing. But it is also a specific point in time. The Day of the Lord refers to the very day that Jesus Christ returns to the Mount of Olives. "On that day his feet will stand on the Mount of Olives, east of Jerusalem, and the Mount of Olives will be split in two from east to west, forming a great valley" (Zechariah 14:4). This will provide a way of escape for those under siege in Jerusalem. In this instance, the "day" refers to that specific moment in time when Christ returns to earth at His second coming.

Near View and Far View

If you go through a concordance and do a study of all the references to the "day of the Lord," "that day," "in that day," the "day for the Lord," and all other related terms, you will find that there is a near view as well as a far view. There is a near view in terms of God's activity in the life of Israel. God was acting on planet Earth on His own behalf in the Babylonian period when He used Babylon to judge His people. He was also at work when He restored Israel from captivity during the times of the Medes and the Persians. The judgment was the Babylonian captivity. The blessing was the restoration of a remnant back into the land as recorded in Ezra, Nehemiah, Haggai, Zechariah, and Malachi. The near view was a Day of the Lord that has already been fulfilled in Israel's history.

But there is also a far view to the Day of the Lord. That is, the Day of the Lord looks beyond the events of the Babylonian captivity and restoration to a climactic time in history that has not yet taken place. The judgment of that future day will take place during the Tribulation and at the end of the Millennium, and the blessing of that future day will be fulfilled in the earthly kingdom of Jesus, Israel's Messiah. If you want to know what the future holds, it holds a day. And that day is called the Day of the Lord.

A WEEK

I described the first portion of the future Day of the Lord as the Tribulation. This period of time is also referred to as a "week." Bible scholars have called it the Seventieth Week of Daniel. Daniel 9:24 says, "Seventy 'sevens' are decreed for your people and your holy city." Seventy "sevens" would be 490 of something. But what are these seventy "sevens"? How is such a phrase to be defined?

The Definition of the Seventy Weeks

The term Daniel used for "seven" is found elsewhere in the Bible, so we can use Scripture to help us interpret Scripture. As recorded in the book of Genesis, Jacob wanted to marry Rachel, the daughter of Laban. But Rachel had an older sister whose name was Leah. Laban made Jacob work seven years for Rachel before he could marry her. However, on the wedding night Laban "slipped Leah under the tent flap"—and you can imagine what occurred that next morning! Jacob had worked seven years for Rachel, but now he found himself married to her "ugly old" sister. When Jacob complained, Laban replied, "It is not our custom here to give the younger daughter in marriage before the older one. Finish this daughter's bridal week; then we will give you the younger one also, in return for another seven years of work" (Genesis 29:26–27). In this passage, the "week" seems to refer to a week of years, or seven years. Jacob had to work seven years before marrying Leah. Then he had to work another seven years for Rachel.

Returning to Daniel 9, seventy "sevens" refer to seventy "sevens" of years. Thus the total time needed to fulfill the prophecy is 490 years. Now we need to do some mathematical calculations. God provided specific markers for dividing up the 490-year period.

> Know and understand this: From the issuing of the decree to restore and rebuild Jerusalem [issued March/April 445 B.C. according to Nehemiah 2:1] until the Anointed One, the ruler, comes, there will be seven "sevens," and sixty-two "sevens." It will be rebuilt with streets and a trench, but in times of trouble. After the sixty-two "sevens," the Anointed One will be cut off and will have nothing. The people of the ruler who will come will destroy the city and the sanctuary. The end will come like a flood: War will continue until the end, and desolations have been decreed. (Daniel 9:25–26)

Seven "sevens" plus sixty-two "sevens" equals sixty-nine "sevens," or 483 years. That is the amount of time that was to pass from the issuing of a command to rebuild Jerusalem until the arrival of the Messiah (the Anointed One). After this period of time, two notable events would take place. The Messiah would be "cut off," or killed, and the city of Jerusalem would be destroyed. This destruction would be at the hands of a group of people who will represent the ruler who will come during the final week of years. Daniel's remarkable prediction is that the 483-year period would end with the arrival of the Messiah. But in the gap between the sixty-ninth and the seventieth weeks, the Messiah would be killed and Jerusalem would be destroyed. The death of Jesus took place in A.D. 33, and the armies of the Roman Empire destroyed the temple in A.D. 70. Sixty-nine of the prophetic "weeks" of years have already been fulfilled, but one seven-year period remains.

The Designs for the Seventieth Week

God revealed to Daniel that this prophetic time period was intended to accomplish certain things in the life of Jerusalem and the Jewish people. Six specific purposes are to be accomplished during the 490 prophetic years. The time period was designed "to finish transgression, to put an end to sin, to atone for wickedness, to bring in everlasting righteousness, to seal up vision and prophecy and to anoint the most holy" (Daniel 9:24). The first three were accomplished at the first coming of Jesus Christ, and the last three will be accomplished at His second coming.

Though it was unknown to those who killed Him, their evil deed was part of God's glorious plan. Christ's death might have looked like the world's darkest hour, but in reality it was God's brightest hour because that event provided a sacrifice for sin. God made it possible for sin no longer to have its ultimate effect. He made it possible for iniquity to be forgiven. He made it possible for atonement to be made for wickedness. These first three purposes for the prophecy found fulfillment in Christ's death on the cross.

But three additional purposes were mentioned in Daniel 9:24. The first was "to bring in everlasting righteousness." The attacks on the World Trade Center and the Pentagon were further reminders that everlasting righteousness has not yet been secured on the face of the earth. Satan walks about this world "like a roaring lion looking for someone to devour" (1 Peter 5:8). He is not yet bound. There is still unrighteousness roaming the earth. Everlasting righteousness has not yet come.

The fifth purpose for the seventy weeks is to "seal up vision and prophecy." In other words, this time period is designed to fulfill all of God's prophetic Scriptures. This is the time when God will bring to completion His prophetic promises. Since there are still prophecies that have not yet been fulfilled, this purpose has not yet happened.

The sixth purpose for the seventy weeks of Israel's prophetic future is to "anoint the most holy." This refers to the holy place in the temple. The temple to which God is referring is the temple that Israel's Messiah will build. There is currently no temple in Israel. Since the first three purposes were accomplished at the first coming of Christ, one must assume that the second set of three will be fulfilled at some point yet future. And since the final "week" of years has not yet taken place, one should expect these purposes to be the focus of that Seventieth Week.

The Division of the Seventieth Week

God divides the final seven-year period into two parts. "He will confirm a covenant with many for one 'seven.' In the middle of the 'seven' he will put an end to sacrifice and offering. And on a wing of the temple he will set up an abomination that causes desolation, until the end that is decreed is poured out on him" (Daniel 9:27). The people who overran Jerusalem in A.D. 70 were the Romans, and verse 26 identifies these people as the ones from whom the "he" of verse 27 will arise. The Dead Sea Scrolls help us understand what is meant by the term "the many." That term is used in their writings to refer to the entire community. As used in Daniel 9:27, the phrase likely is intended to represent all of Israel. It may very well take an international treaty for the Jewish people to be allowed to resume their sacrifices at a temple in Jerusalem.

This coming prince will make a covenant with the nation of Israel, but in the middle of the seven he will put an end to sacrifice and offerings. This event divides the final seven-year period into two halves—the first three-and-a-half years and the last three-and-a-half years. The second half of this period becomes a time of severe persecution for Israel. The time element is repeated in other prophetic passages. In Daniel 12:7 the last half of the Tribulation period, as we have come to know it, is called "a time, times and half a time." "Time" is one year, "times" means two years, and "half a time" is a half a year. The "time of distress" for Israel (12:1) will last three-and-a-half years.

The book of Revelation also speaks of this period of time. In Revelation 11:2 God announced that the Gentiles will trample Jerusalem "for 42 months." In chapter 12 God said that Satan will actively persecute Israel—but that He will act to protect her—"for 1,260 days" (12:6). There are 360 days in a Jewish lunar calendar. Three-and-a-half years would total 42 months or 1,260 days. It seems that the last half of this seven-year period is a time of unparalleled trouble for the nation of Israel.

The Desolations of the Seventieth Week

Two major desolations will take place during this final seven-year period. In the middle of the week, the one who makes a covenant is going to turn on Israel. He is the Antichrist empowered by Satan who "sets himself up in God's temple, proclaiming himself to be God" (2 Thessalonians 2:4). He "will set up an abomination that causes desolation" (Daniel 9:27). That could be his own throne on which he will sit . . . and from which he will claim to be the god of the whole world. Jesus described the same event and called it "the abomination that causes desolation" (Matthew 24:15).

The middle of this seven-year period unleashes a holocaust that will even surpass the horrors carried out by Hitler. The Antichrist will display his wrath against God and against the restored State of Israel. He will hate both, and he will try to steal the glory of their Messiah for himself.

The final part of the seven-year period ends with a second desolation, but this one comes from God and is "poured out" on the evil world ruler. At the end of the Tribulation, the desolator is going to be desolated. The one who is responsible for bringing desolation on Israel will himself experience God's wrath. The Antichrist and his False Prophet will be cast alive into the lake of fire to await their mastermind and empowerer—Satan himself (Revelation 19:20; 20:10). There are two desolations during this seven-year period. One occurs in the middle, and the other happens at the end. The first is against God's people, and the last is against the Enemy of His people.

THE MILLENNIUM

The Millennium is a term used to describe the thousand-year reign of Christ on the earth. It will take place after the Tribulation period and prior to eternity. This is the kingdom era promised throughout the Old Testament. Three components make up the kingdom: the ruler, the realm, and the reign. Who is the ruler, what is the realm, and when is the reign?

The Ruler
Who will be the ultimate ruler? It will be a man from Israel who can rule with God's authority. How will we recognize the rightful ruler? The One who has the right to rule must fulfill five essential roles as prophesied in the Scriptures.

The seed of the woman. The very first prophecy of the Messiah came as an announcement from God to Satan, predicting Satan's ultimate demise at the hands of a human being: "And I will put enmity between you and the woman, and between your offspring and hers; he will crush your head, and you will strike his heel" (Genesis 3:15). A man who is the seed of woman will bring judgment on Satan since the Serpent brought havoc on humanity that had been created by God. The apostle Paul clearly identified Jesus Christ as the fulfillment of this prediction. "But when the time had fully come, God sent his Son, born of a woman" (Galations 4:4). Jesus is the Son of God who was born as a human being. He is the seed of a woman.

Son of Abraham. The ruler must also be a son of Abraham in order to fulfill the Abrahamic covenant. God promised Abraham that it would be through his seed that all the world would be blessed (Genesis 12:3). To be a man from Israel, Jesus had to be a descendant of Abraham, because in God's providence He chose to use the Jewish people to be His channel of blessing to the world.

Son of David. Matthew began his Gospel by establishing Jesus' right to be the King of the Jews. "A record of the genealogy of Jesus Christ the son of David, the son of Abraham" (Matthew 1:1). Then Matthew started from the beginning and tracked forward from Abraham to David (14 generations), from David to the captivity (14 generations), and from the captivity to Christ (14 generations). Matthew recorded the names in the genealogy of Abraham and David to prove Jesus' right to be the King. In order to be the King of the Jews, Jesus had to be from the line of Abraham. But He also had to come from the family of David in order to fulfill the Davidic covenant, which provided for a perpetual kingdom in Israel to be ruled by a descendant of David (2 Samuel 7:13–16). Since Jesus descended from David's line, He has the right to rule. But with what authority does He rule?

Son of Man. Jesus said in His speech on equality with God, "Moreover, the Father judges no one, but has entrusted all judgment to the Son, that all may honor the Son just as they honor the Father. He who does not honor the Son does not honor the Father, who sent him" (John 5:22–23). He continued, "And he [the Father] has given him authority to judge because he is the Son of Man" (v. 27).

The phrase "the Son of Man" is a title Jesus used for Himself when speaking of three separate phases of His ministry: the incarnation and earthly ministry, the passion of His death and resurrection, and His glorification through His ascension and future return. The phrase had messianic overtones as early as Daniel. There the prophet pictured "one like a son of man, coming with the clouds of heaven. . . . He was given authority, glory and sovereign power; all peoples, nations and men of every language worshiped him" (Daniel

7:13–14). God will be justified in His judgment by having His Son execute such judgment since Jesus is also the Son of Man. Equal honor is due Him as it is to the Father.

Son of God. The One who has the right to rule must be a man from Israel who has the right and authority to rule in the kingdom of God. Since it is God's kingdom over which this unique person will rule, He must also be the Son of God. The one question Jesus asked more times than any other in all the New Testament focused attention on His uniqueness as both the Son of Man and the Son of God.

In Matthew 22:41–46, Jesus debated with the Pharisees. "What do you think about the Christ? Whose son is he?" asked Jesus. The leaders from Israel were quick on the trigger. "'The son of David,' they replied." Jesus then pressed, "How is it then that David, speaking by the Spirit, calls him 'Lord'?" Jesus then quoted Psalm 110:1 where David said, "The Lord said to my Lord," and then Jesus asked the leaders, "If then David calls him 'Lord,' how can he be his son?" In other words, if the Messiah will be the Son of David, how can He also be David's Lord?

I love Jesus! He was the ultimate quizmaster, and they didn't know the right answer. The only right answer to Jesus' question is the Virgin Birth. Unless the Son of God had become the Son of Man through the Virgin Birth so that He could be both God and Man, He never could have been David's son and also David's Lord at the same time. Thus Jesus is qualified to be the Ruler over God's kingdom because He, and He alone, is the Man from Israel who has the right to rule with the authority of God.

The Realm

A kingdom is not a kingdom without a realm over which a ruler may rule. What will be the realm over which Jesus will one day rule in sovereign authority? Four concentric circles can be drawn to show four aspects of His realm.

The earth. Out of all the galaxies, God chose the Milky Way. Out of all of the stars and planets in the Milky Way, God chose planet Earth on which to reveal Himself and to send His Son. God's kingdom will cover this earth. The prophet Habakkuk wrote that a time will come when "the earth will be filled with the knowledge of the glory of the LORD, as the waters cover the sea" (Habakkuk 2:14).

The land. Not only is the realm located on planet Earth, but it is also identified with a particular territory—the land of Israel. While God called Abraham and others from beyond the land of Israel, it was to the land of Israel that God asked Abraham to journey. And it was the land of Israel that God promised to Abraham and his descendants. The Lord was born in Bethlehem within the borders of Israel (Micah 5:2), and it will be in Israel that He will establish His kingdom (Ezekiel 45:1–12).

The city. Jerusalem will be the center of activity when the Messiah returns. The city "will be raised up" with all the mountains and valleys in and around the city becoming like a level plain (Zechariah 14:10). Jerusalem will be a very prominent piece of real estate, divided between the portion for the Prince, the portion for the priests, and the site for the future millennial temple. Ezekiel 40–48 provides the detail for the future land and city—components that will be in place when the Messiah rules. The Messiah will establish His kingdom on planet Earth, within the borders of Israel, with His throne firmly centered in Jerusalem.

The temple. Jesus will reign from His throne in fulfillment of the Davidic covenant. And He will supervise the construction of His millennial temple, a project that will be financed internationally. Isaiah 60 describes a time when "the wealth on the seas will be brought to you, to you the riches of the nations will come" (v. 5). Jerusalem's "gates will always stand open, they will never be shut, day or night, so that men may bring you the wealth of the nations" (v. 11).

And this wealth will be used "to adorn the place of my sanctuary" (v. 13). In Haggai 2:8 God announced that "the silver is mine and the gold is mine." God vowed that one day He will shake the heavens and the earth and use the worldly wealth of the nations to glorify Himself in the rebuilt temple.

When I was a boy, the missions offering in the children's department of our little church was collected in a tin bank shaped and painted like a globe. With a childproof closure on the bottom of the bank, the only way to get money out was to turn it over and shake it with the hope that some coins would fall out. It made a terrible racket, and you knew you couldn't steal any of the money, even if you wanted to, because of the built-in alarm system. As I read Haggai 2:8–9, I can almost picture God taking the earth and shaking it upside down to dislodge the silver and gold! But what need does God have for these items? "I will fill this house with glory. . . . And in this place I will grant peace" (Haggai 2:7, 9). Not only will the glory of the Messiah be visible, but also the peace of God finally will be established in Jerusalem.

The Reign

The Bible teaches that Jesus will reign for a thousand years in a righteous kingdom of peace and justice for the ultimate glory of God. Revelation 20:1–7 focuses in a special way on the circumstances of the Messiah's millennial reign over His earthly kingdom.

Chronology. Six times in seven verses, the length of the earthly reign of Messiah is said to be a thousand years. The event that begins the Millennium is the binding and imprisoning of Satan. The purpose stated for this action is to prohibit his deceit of the nations during this time (Revelation 20:3). The fact that people are present in the kingdom who were said to have been martyred in the Tribulation indicates that the Millennium follows the Tribulation period (v. 4). The fact that Satan will be released for a short time to exercise his diabolical influence just before he is cast forever into the lake of fire (v. 10) proves that the Millennium is a definite period of time, since specific events are said to happen on the earth both before and after. The details of the passage are a strong indication that the thousand-year reign of Christ should be taken literally. The Millennium will occur after the Tribulation period and before the season of satanic deception that precedes the Great White Throne judgment (vv. 11–15).

Co-regency. Revelation 20:4 states, "I saw thrones on which were seated those who had been given authority to judge. And I saw the souls of those who had been beheaded because of their testimony for Jesus and because of the word of God. They had not worshiped the beast or his image and had not received his mark on their foreheads or their hands. They came to life and reigned with Christ a thousand years." Now, if those who are resurrected are going to reign with Christ a thousand years, when do they have to come to life? Obviously, after they die. When will they die? The text indicates that it will be during the Tribulation period. If they reign for a thousand years, then their resurrection has to happen prior to the Millennium. "The rest of the dead did not come to life until the thousand years were ended" (v. 5). We are told, therefore, of a resurrection that occurs at the beginning of the thousand-year period and a second resurrection that occurs at the end of the thousand-year period. The second resurrection leads to eternal judgment called the second death. Without the thousand years, you really couldn't separate the resurrections.

A special blessing is announced for those over whom the second death has no power because they were included in the first resurrection. They are called "blessed and holy," and their function is said to be that of "priests of God and of Christ" who "will reign with him for a thousand years" (Revelation 20:6). We thus have a co-regency with Christ and the saints between the two resurrections. The first resurrection is a resurrection unto life, and the second is a resurrection unto death. And between them is a period of time when the saints will rule with the Messiah here on earth.

	Judgment Seat of Christ	Judgment of the Nations		Great White Throne Judgment
	7 Yr Tribulation		1000 Yr Earthly Kingdom	
Rapture		2nd Coming		Satan Released
1st Resurrection				2nd Resurrection

The next event on the calendar of prophecy is the rapture of the church. This is that event whereby "the dead in Christ will rise first. After that, we who are still alive and are left will be caught up together with them to meet the Lord in the air. And so we will be with the Lord forever (cf 1 Thess 4:13-17). What happens after the rapture of the church? The judgment seat of Christ in heaven. There is some question as to whether this judgment happens immediately or whether it stretches throughout the time the earth is experiencing the tribulation. Following the rapture will be the seven-year period of tribulation. We've already seen that in the middle of that "week of years" there will be an abomination of desolation which divides the week into two halves of three-and-a-half years each. The tribulation will culminate with the judgments that accompany the second coming of Christ. The beast and the false prophet will be thrown into the lake of fire by Christ Himself. Prior to the beginning of the millennium will be a resurrection and after the millennium will be a resurrection. The first will take place in connection with the Judgment of the Nations (Sheep and Goats) to judge the wicked and to provide for the righteous to enter the kingdom in fulfillment of the covenant promises.

The church comes back with Christ at His second coming

according to Revelation 19:7, 8. We as the church, along with those others, reign with Him for a thousand years. During this period Satan is bound and imprisoned. At the end of a thousand years Satan will be released for a short time. He will lead his final rebellion of deceit and disobedience and then be cast into the lake of fire. The final judgment of human history is called the Great White Throne Judgment. At that judgment the wicked of all the ages will stand before Christ as their Judge. They will be shown by both their works and their lack of faith that their eternal judgment will be just. Everyone whose name is not written in the book of life is thrown into the lake of fire. (Rev 20:14). The Great White Throne Judgment finishes this whole sequence prior to the consummation in eternity. This is the big picture.

Consummation. First Corinthians 15 is not the last chapter in the Bible, but it records the last events of human history prior to eternity. The apostle Paul wrote,

> But Christ has indeed been raised from the dead, the first-fruits of those who have fallen asleep. For since death came through a man, the resurrection of the dead comes also through a man. For as in Adam all die, so in Christ all will be made alive. But each in his own turn: Christ, the firstfruits; then, when he comes, those who belong to him. (1 Corinthians 15:20–23)

When Christ returns for His church, all church-age believers will be resurrected or raptured to meet Him in the air (1 Thessalonians 4:13–18). When He comes at His second advent to the earth, there will be a resurrection of Old Testament saints and Tribulation saints who will rise to meet Him and be evaluated for life in the kingdom.

Paul then looked forward to the climax of this earth.

> Then the end will come, when he hands over the kingdom to God the Father after he has destroyed all dominion,

109

authority and power. For he must reign until he has put all his enemies under his feet. The last enemy to be destroyed is death. For he "has put everything under his feet." Now when it says that "everything" has been put under him, it is clear that this does not include God himself, who put everything under Christ. When he has done this, then the Son himself will be made subject to him who put everything under him, so that God may be all in all. (1 Corinthians 15:24–28)

What is the ultimate testimony of human history? God has the right to be God over everything and everyone. The angels who rebelled against Him are going to find out they were wrong. Humans who rebelled against Him are going to find out they were wrong. The Beast, the False Prophet, Satan, death, and hades all go into the lake of fire. And then Jesus will hand the kingdom back to God the Father. That is where history is headed. That is what the future holds.

CONCLUSION

As the year 2000 approached, prophets of doom predicted worldwide catastrophe. Some saw religious significance in the beginning of a new millennium. Others saw technological destruction as Y2K threatened to bring all computers to a halt. I had never preached through the book of Revelation, so I decided to preach a series called "WYN-TKAY2K—What You Need to Know About Y2K."

I will never forget what God did in my heart when I prepared to preach Revelation 4–5. I was reminded that God provides us with a picture of the Judge before He describes the judgments (chaps. 6–18), and I learned a profound truth: Those who begin the song of worship—the four living creatures, the twenty-four elders, and the thousands and thousands of angels—have been with God from the beginning of time. And yet, when they gather before God's throne in the future, they are still in awe of Him. What is it about God that, even for the angels, has never gotten old? It is His glory, His majesty, His power, His dominion, His character, and His authority that, for all eternity, will impress them . . . and us. He is worthy of all worship!

Billy Sunday, the great evangelist of the early twentieth century, captured best the reality of life "from here to eternity."

Twenty-nine years ago I entered at the portico of Genesis and walked down the corridor of the Old Testament art galleries where pictures of Noah and Abraham and Joseph and Moses, Isaac and Jacob and Daniel hung on the wall. I passed into the music room of the Psalms where the Spirit sweeps the keyboard of nature until it seems that every reed and pipe in God's great organ responds to the harp of David, the sweet singer of Israel. I entered the chamber of Ecclesiastes where the voice of the preacher is heard and into the conservatory of Sharon and the lily of the valley where sweet spices filled and perfumed my life. I entered into the business office of Proverbs and on into the observatory of the Prophets where I saw telescopes of various sizes pointing to far-off events, concentrating on the Bright and Morning Star, which was to arise above the moon-lit hills of Judea, for our salvation and our redemption. I entered into the audience room of the King of kings, catching a vision written by Matthew, Mark, Luke, and John, and thence into the correspondence room with Paul and Peter and James and John writing their epistles. And I stepped into the throne room of Revelation, where tower the glittering peaks, where sits the King of kings upon His throne of glory, with the healing of the nations in His hand. And I cried out, "All hail the power of Jesus' name, let angels prostrate fall and bring forth that royal diadem and crown Him Lord of All!"

NOTE

1. Adapted from: Mark Hitchcock, *101 Answers to Most Asked Questions About The End Times*, (Sisters, OR: Multnomah Publishers Inc., 2001), 160-161.

6 HOW SHOULD WE THEN LIVE?

Dr. Larry Mercer

November 12, 2001, was an important day in the life of Navy Petty Officer Ruben Rodriguez. At the age of thirty-two, he was in the prime of his life. He had just completed a seven-month tour of duty with the U.S.S. *Enterprise*. The *Enterprise* was the first U.S. carrier deployed in the war on terrorism launched after September 11.

He boarded flight 587, along with 259 other people, leaving JFK International Airport in New York City, with the expectation of meeting his wife and children in the Dominican Republic later that same day. His three-year-old son was waiting at home with excitement and anticipation of his arrival. He was headed home to a waiting family.

Then the unexpected—and for a long period of time the unexplainable—happened. Literally, less than two minutes after the plane took off, his dreams and his plans of spending time that day with family and friends went up in smoke as the plane he was riding on careened into the ground.

Nobody anticipated that this ordinary person—and 259 others—with ordinary dreams and ordinary plans would die such an extraordinary death. When Ruben Rodriguez boarded that plane, he had the perspective that his life was under his control. But he soon realized that his life was not really under his control after all.

Michael Gaines serves in the National Guard. I've known him for a number of years. He and Rhonda are devoted parents and followers of Jesus Christ. They built a family business that enabled them to do a lot of good things for their family and make a significant impact on their church and their community. Everything was going well for them until the attacks on the World Trade Center and the Pentagon. In the subsequent military buildup, Michael was called to active duty. And Michael and Rhonda soon learned that their lives—which they thought were under control—were not really under their control after all.

Thomas Morris served as a postal employee for a number of years. He faithfully worked for the Brentwood branch of the United States Post Office in Washington, D.C. He had a very solid reputation among his colleagues at work, his fellow church members, and his community. Then, on November 7, he became so ill that he called 911. As he described how he was feeling, and the condition of his body, his symptoms alerted emergency personnel, medical professionals, and, eventually, postal officials to what finally was diagnosed to be anthrax. Unfortunately, it soon led to his death.

Thomas Morris never imagined that in the process of performing his normal duties—tasks that after more than thirty years on the job had become routine—he would ever come into deadly contact with anthrax. He was another ordinary person doing an ordinary job . . . only to die at the hands of an unknown enemy acting on motives we do not understand. He thought his life was under his control, but sadly, he finally discovered that his life was not under his control after all.

THE ILLUSION OF PERSONAL CONTROL

Each one of the three people described above began the fateful day that radically changed his life assuming he had control over his destiny. And in many ways we are just like them. We are ordinary people, living out our ordinary lives, but assuming that those lives are under our complete control. And then events like those on September 11 shatter our complacency and make us realize that we don't have our lives completely under our control after all.

Unfortunately, some individuals still awaken each morning believing the appealing lie stated so eloquently by William Ernest Henley at the end of his poem "Invictus": "I am the master of my fate. I am the captain of my soul." But after the major events that rocked our world the final few months of 2001, anyone who believes he or she is "the master of my fate" or "captain of my soul" is piloting a paper boat. When that person reaches eternity, he or she will discover that they have been trying to write the script for a Hollywood movie. But the real world isn't Hollywood.

And that raises a question that many are asking, though they may voice it in different ways. Some might ask, "How could God allow such evil and suffering to happen in the world?" Others would voice the question this way, "How could a good God allow innocent people to suffer and die?"

Ask God the Proper Question

These questions beg for an answer, but in this life God has not chosen always to give us a complete answer. God sometimes places us in the uncomfortable position of having to trust Him even when we don't understand. And we often become frustrated because we started with the wrong question. Instead of asking, "Why did You allow this to happen?" we ought to be asking, "How should I live in light of the events around me?"

God has the sovereign right to exercise the privilege of Deity. He has placed us in the position of being the *servants* rather than the *Sovereign*. Our lack of complete control over our lives reminds us that we are the *creatures* rather than the *Creator*. God alone determines what will come to pass, and He isn't required to give us an explanation.

To gain a proper perspective on life, the very first thing we need to do is learn to ask the proper question. That is, rather than fixating on the question "Why?" we need to ask the question, "How should we then live?" In effect, we need to say, "God, I surrender to the fact that You are the Creator and I am the creature. I surrender to the fact that You are the Sovereign and I am the servant. I surrender to the fact that I am not in complete control of my own life." Only when we arrive at a point where we can accept—even embrace—God's complete control over our lives, can we move from asking "why" to asking "how."

Acknowledge God's Complete Control

How should we live when the illusion of complete personal control has been snatched from our hands? We should seek to live in a way that will please God. Our lack of complete personal control over our lives is illustrated every day. Try to control traffic, the weather, the actions of family, friends, or colleagues. If we think about it, it's quite clear that we don't control our own destiny. But the events of September 11 caught our attention in a unique way. Why? Perhaps because our illusion of personal control was shattered by people we do not know, who live in places most of us have not visited, and who have deep convictions we do not understand. Where do we find help?

THE ANSWERS FROM GOD'S WORD

Local and national news programs help us stay abreast of current events, but they cannot give us answers to life's deepest questions about how to live in light of prophecy. So where can we go to find such answers? God has given us a resource that can help all of us navigate the challenges of our world . . . and that can give us answers to life's deepest mysteries. That resource is the Bible. The Scriptures give us God's insight on how to deal with the challenges of the world.

One passage that offers great insight is 1 Thessalonians 5:1–11. In the passage, the apostle Paul shared God's program for the future. And he also explained how knowledge of God's Word can give comfort to those facing intense personal struggles. As we look at this text, it is clear that these believers were living in a time of high anxiety. All around them people were engaged in futile speculation. Paul began by reminding these people that, although God had not told them everything, there were some very specific truths He had given . . . and in which they could put great confidence.

This passage helps us see that once we have the illusion of personal self-control snatched from our hands, we are then in a position where God can speak to us. He can do so because we are not operating under the pretense of self-sufficiency. Instead, we realize that our lives are in His hands.

Be Alert

Paul wants his readers to be alert to this one simple truth: God has a plan for human history. God was not caught by surprise by the traumatic events of September 11. First Thessalonians 5 helps us be alert to the reality of God's plan. In this passage, the apostle Paul gave his readers insights into a specific time in God's prophetic timetable— but he did so in a way that has great application both for his original readers and for us today. The key to comfort is understanding that God has human history under control. History is nothing more than *His* story!

Those who do not know Jesus Christ as their personal Lord and Savior are left to bite their nails and wring their hands when the unforeseen happens, because they cannot figure out what is really taking place in the world around them. But God has given His children clear direction and instruction in His Word. He has a plan for human history, and He has even revealed the overall prophetic timetable for that plan in the Bible.

There are many references to the end times in Scripture. Often that period is introduced by the phrase "the last days." Although God has not provided the exact date for the start of the "last days," He has assured us of the certainty of that time period. So what does the fact of God's plan for the future have to do with believers? The answer is: a great deal . . . if we are fully aware of His plan.

Be Aware

The very first thing Paul reminded the believers in Thessalonica was that he didn't need to write to them "about times and dates . . . for you know very well" (1 Thessalonians 5:1–2). What were they so aware of? The following verses indicate that they understood the events associated with the "day of the Lord." They were aware that God had a plan and that, in spite of the evil acts of humans, history is moving along a path God marked out in eternity past. Paul underscored six very clear messages in 1 Thessalonians 5:1–3. Each of those messages reminds us of the importance of remaining aware of God's plan.

Awareness of God's plan helps us understand how to live today. The Thessalonian believers had demonstrated a "deep conviction" to the message of God preached through Paul. Their "faith in God" became "known everywhere" as they "turned to God from idols to serve the living and true God, and to wait for his Son from heaven, whom he raised from the dead—Jesus, who rescues us from the coming wrath" (1 Thessalonians 1:5–11). Evidently, Paul had told them about God's plan for the future. It is no accident that every chapter of this book ends with a reference to the coming of Christ. Our challenge is to mimic the pattern of the Thessalonian believers in knowledge, passion, and lifestyle so our lives are worthy of the same type of commendation.

In chapter 4 Paul reminded the believers that Christ will return to gather together those believers who had already died as well as those who were still alive. This event is often referred to as the Rapture of the church. Paul then made this truth applicable to the "here and now" as he urged them to "encourage each other with these words" (4:18). Our knowledge of what the future holds should make a difference in how we live today.

Awareness of God's plan reminds us that this present earth is not our final home. Paul also reminded his readers that this earth is not their final home. This life is a pilgrimage, not our ultimate destination. The fact that this earth is not the final stop for believers keeps us from adopting the philosophy of the hedonists who say, "Let us eat and drink, for tomorrow we die" (1 Corinthians 15:32). If this earth was the final stop for us as believers, then the challenges of our world could easily tempt us to live only for this moment. But the Scriptures make it clear that, for the believer, eternity calls.

When the Bible describes the second coming of Jesus, it does so in a way that reminds us of the truth that God will someday judge all the evil that has been perpetuated throughout human history and will establish a time when one called "Faithful and True" will arrive to rule "with an iron scepter" (Revelation 19:11, 15). As the earlier writers in this book made clear, the Rapture of the church will occur at least seven years before the second coming of Christ.

Although we don't know the time when Christ will come for His church—or when He will return to the earth to rule as King of Kings—we can have confidence in the certainty of His future involvement through the Rapture and Second Coming. And we know that our final destination is to "be with the Lord forever" (1 Thessalonians 4:17).

Having reminded his readers of their eternal destination, Paul then described the judgment that will come on this earth following the Rapture. Once again, God exercises His privilege as the Sovereign Lord of history. Paul makes it clear that while the event is certain and imminent, the exact timing is known only to God. To the world, the events will be as sudden and unexpected as "a thief in the night" (5:2). But we know in advance, because God has shared that knowledge with us.

Awareness of God's plan helps us keep our hearts turned toward eternity rather than being distracted by the trappings of time. When I was growing up, my mom would leave us at home with some chores to do. After outlining our responsibilities while she was gone, she would say, "I'll be back at 5:00." I would immediately calculate how much time I thought it would take to complete the job. If I expected the task to take fifteen minutes, guess when I would start? That's right . . . 4:45! If I knew when she was coming, I would wait until the last possible minute to begin.

OK, I admit the quality of my work suffered because I did not always calculate the correct amount of time the job deserved. And, I am ashamed to admit, I would often try to cover up my procrastination by saying, "Oh, Mom, I've been working the whole time!" Then one day Mom left and told me she would be home at 3:00. But she finished her shopping early . . . and walked through the door at 2:45. It wasn't pretty!

I learned a valuable lesson from that experience. I only stayed in a state of constant readiness when I did not know the exact time my mother was coming home. I'm convinced that God knows we are prone to spiritual procrastination. Had He revealed the exact time when His prophetic program was to begin, then we would be prone to get comfortable, to procrastinate, to allow ourselves less time than we really need to accomplish His work. It was not pretty when my mother came home earlier than I expected. It will be even worse if God comes back and discovers that we have not been about His business for our lives. That is why Paul wrote, "So then, let us not be like others, who are asleep, but let us be alert and self-controlled" (1 Thessalonians 5:6).

Awareness of God's plan helps us guard against becoming too complacent and comfortable in this life. We must guard against complacency and comfort because they are lethal to the spiritual life of a believer. Or, to use the story that inspired a book by the same title, we must avoid becoming the frog in the kettle. Do you remember the story? If you put a frog in a kettle of boiling water, he will immediately jump out. But if you put a frog in a kettle of cold water on the stove and slowly turn up the heat, it will remain "comfortable" and will stay in the water. As you increase the temperature slowly, almost imperceptibly, you can literally cook the frog to death.

Satan understands that if he can get us to feel comfortable in the world, he can gradually dial up the heat of his allurement and temptation until we succumb to his evil ways. We must remember that this is not our home; this is not the final stop on our journey. That is why Paul reminded his readers that the final end of this earth is judgment and destruction. "While people are saying, 'Peace and safety,' destruction will come on them suddenly, as labor pains on a pregnant woman, and they will not escape" (5:3).

Having described the judgment coming on the world, Paul then reminded his readers that they share a different destiny. "But you, brothers, are not in darkness so that this day should surprise you like a thief. You are all sons of the light and sons of the day. We do not belong to the night or to the darkness" (vv. 4–5). This is huge because it forces us to see the danger of complacency. If we get too comfortable, we relax a little bit too much. We sit back and assume that everything is just fine. "I'm paying my bills, and everybody is healthy. I have a nice house and a nice car. Everything seems to be going great."

Awareness of God's plan keeps us from being surprised by evil. Paul quickly reminded his readers that they must avoid a wrong response. He tells them they are "not in darkness," but he also lets them know that darkness does exist. What is darkness? In the Bible, darkness symbolizes the absence of God. It represents evil. It is a picture of judgment. It is a symbol of spiritual blindness . . . and death. Those who don't know Jesus Christ as their personal Savior are in darkness. They are spiritually blind. They have the absence of light. And they are sometimes characterized by evil.

The evening news is a commentary on the darkness of our world. It is a graphic visualization of the absence of God in many places in our communities. And Paul reminded the believers at Thessalonica that darkness does exist. Why is this important? It's important because Christians often react naively when confronted with evil. "Oh, my goodness! There's darkness! I can't believe it!" Because we have come to the light, we sometimes forget that this world still lives in darkness. This side of eternity, darkness will continue to exist in the world.

Awareness of God's plan motivates us to be light-bearers. But what is the real problem? It is not just the presence of darkness . . . it is also the absence of light. Pay close attention to what I just said. God wants people who can look at the darkness and then say, "I'm going to pierce the darkness in the name of Jesus." You see, many people are great thermometers, but few know what it means to be a thermostat.

Do you understand the difference? A thermometer is an instrument that excels at telling the temperature, at reflecting conditions as they actually exist. It's easy to be a thermometer, but it's much more difficult to be a thermostat. A thermostat is an instrument that not only reads the temperature but also acts to change the temperature. Paul wanted the Thessalonians to understand that darkness exists and that we are not part of that darkness. But then Paul took these believers from being complacent thermometers to being active thermostats. "You are all sons of the light and sons of the day" (1 Thessalonians 5:5).

How shall we then live? How shall we respond to what is happening around us? We should be light. And what does light do? Light exposes darkness. Light symbolizes the presence of God. Light represents all that is good. God is calling each of us to be a light-bearer. In our homes. In our churches. In our communities. In our places of work. God wants us to recognize that we are not of the darkness; we are of the light.

How can someone make a difference if he or she is asleep? That is why Paul commanded, "So then, let us not be like others, who are asleep, but let us be alert and self-controlled" (v. 6). There are people all around who don't know Jesus. They have no hope, no eternal perspective. They see the events happening all around, but they think that what is happening is an accident, not something that is under the control of the providential hand of God. They don't have a sense about how to make sense of the world. And yet, God has given us the light so that we would be light-bearers. So how should we live? Jesus said it best. "You are the light of the world. . . . In the same way, let your light shine before men, that they may see your good deeds and praise your Father in heaven" (Matthew 5:14, 16).

Be Assured
Be assured of God's promise. Our challenge is to live out

who and what we are in the midst of a dark and dying world. But how can we do that if we are afraid? And that leads to the next point in the passage that is so very important. Not only do we need to be aware and alert, but we must also be assured. "For God did not appoint us to suffer wrath but to receive salvation through our Lord Jesus Christ" (1 Thessalonians 5:9). Paul reminded his readers that God has not destined believers to the time of wrath that he just said would come on the earth. Paul had earlier told these believers that God's plan for them, through Jesus, was to rescue them "from the coming wrath" (1:10). This time of wrath is that period of time often called the Tribulation period. And Paul wanted to assure these believers that their destiny did not include that period of time. Believers on this earth can expect to experience tribulation. But we are not destined to go through the Tribulation period . . . that special time of worldwide judgment just prior to the second coming of Christ.

First Thessalonians 5:9 also gives us a window of understanding into what God said in Psalm 121. The psalmist first looked at the hills and mountains that stood between his home and his destination—Jerusalem. The hills contained rocky pathways, unknown obstacles, wild animals, and men of treachery. When the psalmist first gazed at the towering sentinels blocking his journey, he asked, "Where will I get the help I need to make it through?" But then he immediately answered his own question. "My help comes from the God who made these mountains!" Nothing can happen in the life of the believer that is not first of all filtered through the will of God. No matter how much we worry, no matter how much we fret, it won't change God's ability to protect us as He promised.

We must remember that God has a filter around our lives. Whatever the Enemy tries to pour out on us, God will only allow that which He has already planned for our lives to come through. Does this mean we can be careless? No, we need to walk in wisdom. Does it mean we can be irresponsible? No, God wants us to live responsibly. But as we seek to live carefully and responsibly, we can say, "God, my life is in Your hands. I will no longer wake up in the middle of the night, anxious that something bad might happen to me. I know You are able to protect me."

The psalmist ended Psalm 121 by assuring his readers that "the LORD will watch over your coming and going" (v. 8). That phrase, by the way, is a Hebrew expression intended to picture the totality of God's protection. He watches over those *coming* to worship Him in Jerusalem, and He also watches over those *going* home. From beginning to end, there is no dimension of our experience that can enter our lives without passing through God's divine filter. That promise gives me a great sense of security. The psalmist also described God as the One who "will neither slumber nor sleep" (v. 4). God is on guard twenty-four hours a day! He is watching over my life and protecting me from all harm. And He never goes off duty!

Be assured of God's purpose. Having reminded his readers of God's promise, Paul then focused on God's purpose: "He died for us so that, whether we are awake or asleep, we may live together with him" (1 Thessalonians 5:10). God has an eternal purpose for our lives, and it will not be fully revealed until the day we see our Savior. Sometimes we get so enamored with the toys of time that we forget the treasures of eternity. "I don't want to die! I don't want to die!" But guess what? Psalm 116 says, "Precious in the sight of the LORD is the death of his saints" (v. 15). For the believer, death is not a period; it's a comma. It's not the end; it's only the beginning. The moment life on earth ceases, life in heaven begins. Physically, death brings temporary separation from our friends, but it allows us to experience eternal life in the presence of a loving, holy God. And although, from a purely human perspective, none of us wants to leave the fellowship of our family and friends, or to give up the toys of time, when we finally get to heaven, none of us will regret having traded them in for the treasures of eternity. We must shift our focus from time to eternity. We must remember that someday we will "live together with him." That is our assurance from God.

Harry Ironside was traveling to a funeral, and a little boy was riding in the car with him. The boy asked Dr. Ironside to explain death. Just as the little boy posed the question, a big truck passed by and its shadow passed across the car. Ironside, the great communicator and illustrator, said, "Son, for the believer death is like the shadow that hit the car. But for the nonbeliever death is like the truck." You see, when the shadow of death brushes past the believer, it is just a passing glance . . . just a fading moment as the believer is ushered from time into eternity. But for the nonbeliever there is the sudden finality of a Christless eternity with no hope, no help, just the eternal horror of the lake of fire.

Be Active

God want us to be aware, to be alert, and to be assured of His protection. And then there is one final point that the text gives us. Paul ended in 1 Thessalonians 5:11 by stating that God also wants His children to be active. "Therefore encourage one another and build each other up, just as in fact you are doing." How should we then live? We should be active in personal ministry. This is no time to engage in paralysis by analysis, being afraid to act unless we are completely sure what is going to happen. To live in this way is to go through life as a spectator, turning on the television, following what is happening, wondering what is going on, trying to determine what will happen next. And during all the time that we sit and watch, the clock is ticking, time is slipping away . . . and people are dying and going into a Christless eternity. Once we are aware of God's master plan for history, once we finally understand that we are not of the darkness, once we realize that God has a filter over our lives—and that nothing can break through unless permitted by Him—then we must actively work to encourage and build up believers . . . and reach out in love to those who don't know Jesus Christ.

WHAT SHOULD I DO?

World War II brought tremendous destruction to Germany. Many of that nation's cathedrals were destroyed during the Allied bombing campaigns. When the war was over, most cities and towns began the painstaking process of trying to restore the things that had once been so special to them. In one town, the people decided to rebuild the cathedral and restore a statue of Christ that had stood in front of it. They rebuilt the cathedral, and it was beautiful. They then called in the best artists and craftsmen to restore the statue of Christ.

Before the statue had been destroyed, a small plaque had been attached on the front that read, "Whosoever will, let him come." As they began the restoration, everything went well until they tried to reconstruct the part of the statue where Christ's hands had been. In spite of their best efforts, they didn't believe the hands could be sufficiently repaired to do justice to the statue. Finally, one of the artists said, "Let's not try to restore the hands." So they placed the statue back in front of the cathedral—a beautiful statue of Christ, but without hands. They also changed the plaque on the front of the statue to read, "Christ has no hands but ours."

As you finish this book, lift up your eyes and look out on a world that is desperate and discouraged, concerned and confused. In many ways, our world is as shattered and broken as that statue in front of the cathedral in Germany.

Now realize that Christ has no hands but yours to reach out to this world. If you know Jesus Christ as your Savior, then He expects you to be active for Him. The time might be short, but use what time He gives you to make an eternal difference in others' lives.

But as you look out on the world, also take time to examine your own heart. Up to this point, I have assumed that you know Jesus Christ as your Savior. But only you know whether or not He is a reality in your life. If you have never experienced forgiveness for your sins, then you are still among those who are destined for God's wrath. I cannot close this chapter without telling the eternal good news about Jesus Christ. My hope for heaven is not grounded in my education, my economic condition, or my ethnicity. It is grounded in my personal relationship with Jesus Christ. Let me tell you some simple, but eternally significant, realities.

The Bible declares that all of us are sinners. Romans 3:23 says, "For all have sinned and fall short of the glory of God." Unfortunately, sin has eternal consequences and separates us from God. Romans 6:23 says, "For the wages of sin is death, but the gift of God is eternal life in Christ Jesus our Lord." We cannot save ourselves. The price to be paid for sin is death. But that is where the good news of Jesus Christ enters the equation. When He died on the cross, He did so to pay the penalty for our sin. Romans 5:8 says, "But God demonstrates his own love for us in this: While we were still sinners, Christ died for us."

How does one receive the forgiveness of sin that comes from Christ's death on the cross? We receive it in simple faith by recognizing what God has done for us and by placing our trust in Jesus Christ and His death on our behalf. Ephesians 2:8–9 says, "For it is by grace you have been saved, through faith—and this not from yourselves, it is the gift of God—not by works, so that no one can boast." If you have not made a personal decision to trust Jesus Christ as your Savior, please don't miss the opportunity to do so right now. Pause just for a moment, open your heart to God, and pray in your heart something like the following prayer.

> Dear Father,
> I know that I have sinned and done things that have separated me from You. I believe You sent Your Son, Jesus Christ, to earth to die on the cross to pay the penalty for my sin; and that you raised Him from the dead to prove that His payment was sufficient. Right now, I want to place my trust in Jesus Christ, as the substitute for my sin. Please forgive me and give me eternal life. I ask this in Christ's name. Amen.

This is a simple prayer with profound implications. And if you prayed it, then discuss your decision with someone whom you know to be a Christian. If you don't know anyone, then look for a church in your area where the Bible is believed and taught, and tell your decision to that pastor. And start reading the Bible, because in its pages you will learn more about God, and about His Son, Jesus Christ. After all, Jesus Christ might return to take you home to heaven at any time!

Moody Press, a ministry of Moody Bible Institute,
is designed for education, evangelization, and edification.
If we may assist you in knowing more about Christ
and the Christian life, please write us without obligation:
Moody Press, c/o MLM, Chicago, Illinois 60610.